Healing

Heart

and

Soul

Healing

Heart

and

Soul

with meditation
commentaries by
Margaret Pinkerton

Dr Roger Cole

Lothian
BOOKS

Thomas C. Lothian Pty Ltd
132 Albert Road, South Melbourne, Victoria 3205

Text copyright © Roger Cole 2001
Meditation commentaries copyright © B K Media Pty Ltd 2001

First published 2001
Reprinted 2002

National Library of Australia
Cataloguing-in-Publication data:

Cole, Roger, 1955– .
    Healing Heart and Soul.

    ISBN 0 7344 0213 9.

    I. Meditation. 2. Mental healing. 3. Spiritual healing.
    I. Pinkerton, Margaret. II. Title.

291.435

Designed by Tou-Can Design
Typeset by Caz Brown
Cover image by Michael Mucci Design
Back cover photograph by Peter Damo
Printed in Australia by Griffin Press

contents

Part Two — Inner healing and self-transformation

acknowledgements

In writing this book I am particularly grateful
to Margaret Pinkerton for her wisdom, purity and
inspiration. Margaret, knowing you has been a
blessing, enabling me to develop new strengths
through your faith and understanding of the soul.

The Brahma Kumaris World Spiritual University
has suffused my character with love and compassion
over the last decade, teaching me to be peaceful
and benevolent while giving me a way of looking
at the world with renewed confidence and respect.
Royalties from the sale of this book are dedicated
to the worldwide service of this organisation and its
teachings of Raja Yoga meditation. I am indebted
to Baba, and thankful for teachers such as Dadi
Janki and Didi Nirmala whose discipline and purity
empower others.

As always I send my love and thanks to the

many patients who have shared their living and dying with me. They have awakened me to the truth of our immortality. Also to my colleagues from the many disciplines that make up palliative care — thank you for being pioneers and sharing the dream. You know we make a difference.

And to Sue, Sam and Lucinda, thanks for being just as you are.

introduction

Several years ago I met a couple after speaking on meditation with an Indian Yogi. I was standing in the lecture hall as people left when Sue and Brian approached me. Sue told me about the loss they had experienced after their twin boys, Jason and Stephen, were born. Sadly, both babies were very sick when born and Stephen died when only a few days old. Sue told me the sense of loss was overwhelming, but she commented on how supportive the hospital staff were. After leaving hospital Sue suffered a protracted state of grief and despair that no one else seemed to understand. Her family expected her to be happy that she still had Jason and to get on with life. But she had panic attacks during the day and nightmares at night. She was depressed and afraid to go out and cried frequently. She pined for Stephen, the child she had lost, and felt that she was neglecting Jason. Furthermore, counselling hadn't helped her.

'Why isn't there something more for a couple like us?' she asked me, pleading. 'A support group — anything?'

'Sue, what happened was terrible for you both, and grief is difficult to understand. But there are so many traumatic events in the world — it seems that everyone needs someone else's help. For every type of loss there is one or another support group and while these may help they will never be the answer. We need to learn to look within, to find truth and to understand what we experience in a more enlightened way.'

This is not my usual way of responding to someone in despair. Perhaps it was due to the spiritual atmosphere that followed the Yogi's talk. Perhaps it was intuition or simply that I was touched to respond meaningfully.

'Do you mean I should think of it as something that was meant to be?' Sue asked.

'Not exactly. Think of yourself as a soul and that Brian, Stephen and Jason are also eternal, living spirits. I believe the four of you are connected and that Stephen never died. In the short time his spirit was with you he was fulfilled, even while in the womb.' I went on to share my belief that souls who 'leave early' have had a short stabilising birth in which they experience the love of a particular family. 'Stephen needed your love briefly, before he moved on to another life. You must have known him in the past and will meet him again in the future.'

As I was speaking I noticed a visible change in Sue and Brian. Their faces became lighter and happier. They were almost euphoric, giving me the confidence to say as much as I had. Sue said she felt that a huge burden had just been lifted. Her comment made me realise what had happened. I had helped them to realise a relationship that they felt deprived of; a purpose for Stephen's life and a meaning for his existence. Their pain had been healed in one moment of spiritual clarity and understanding. They had found peace.

This book is written for Sue, Brian, Jason and souls like them. People who are seeking answers through truth, understanding and enlightenment. It is written to help those who have suffered, who wish to let go of their pain; and for those who are burdened by their past.

The meditation commentaries will appeal to those who seek peace and refuge from a world that is too fast, stressful and chaotic. Their wisdom will calm you and give your mind strength, confidence and clarity, which you can use to bring peace to the lives of your friends and relatives. If you are already spiritual and want to develop your spirituality in a practical way, they will enable you to sustain inner peace and remain beyond negative influences; to love unconditionally through your greatest asset — the power of your mind. The meditation commentaries are available on the CD *Healing Heart and Soul* which is designed to take you into a deeper meditation experience. The CD is available from Brahma Kumaris Raja Yoga Centres listed in the back of the book.

Part One will take you deeper into the understanding and practice of meditation outlined in my first book, *Mission of Love*. It is recommended as a study for inner healing and self-transformation. Whether you read it quickly or study it a lesson at a time is up to you. A committed and disciplined approach to the study of the text and regular use of the meditation commentaries offers the greatest benefit.

Part Two is designed as a sixty-day meditation course to awaken your highest potential through healing your heart and soul. This book explores the way spirituality and truth are connected to healing and I have included our healing relationship with God. For the idea of God I, invite you to substitute

words that better describe your own beliefs and
ideals. Although the God I see is beyond gender,
I have used conventional terminology for the
convenience and flow of the text. So let us begin
with the reawakening of innocence.

healing

heart

and

soul

reawakening

innocence

healing your heart and soul

*H*ealing your heart means healing your emotions, whereas healing the soul concerns our sense of identity. These two are intimately linked. When your heart is healed, you experience love and happiness and you feel hopeful and enthusiastic. When your soul is healed you experience unity and enduring peace as your spiritual identity awakens. When both are healed you have deep love and understanding, a feeling of brotherhood or sisterhood and a vocation to extend this love and understanding to the world.

When something good happens, such as passing a test, we enjoy the moment but quickly forget it. On the other hand bad or devastating events linger and are difficult to forget. This is a challenge for the Heart. It holds on to the memories that create feelings of anger, jealousy, dislike or sadness. The Heart then communicates its sadness and regret to the Mind. 'I feel so unhappy when I remember what happened that I want to forgive and forget.'

But the Mind says, 'No! I won't let you forget.'
Sometimes the Mind doesn't even listen to the
Heart; it just keeps the Heart feeling resentful.
Then the Heart and Mind conspire against the
Soul. 'Forget about the Soul,' says the Mind.
'There are only the two of us here and we must
work together to get what we want.' When the
Heart and Mind form this alliance we forget we
are souls.

The Mind is also cunning. When it can no
longer stand the tension or distress of unhappy
memories, it makes a deal with the Heart. 'Okay,
let's forgive and forget, and get on with life.' But
it fools the heart by secretly concealing its painful
memories in the subconscious, where they
reawaken when triggered by particular words or
circumstances. Because the Heart is more honest
and naive than the Mind, it feels vulnerable and
challenged without understanding why. But the
Mind didn't mean to deceive, it just took a
precaution, keeping the hurtful memories stored
away for future reference. 'So we don't get hurt
again,' it reasons, but it doesn't let the Heart know
how vulnerable it is. Bit by bit the Heart and Mind
separate themselves from the Soul as they fashion
a personality based on fear and past experiences.

Inner healing begins when the Heart and Mind

begin to work together; when the Mind starts to listen to the Heart and confide in it.

'There is so much love inside you; I had forgotten that. We both want peace and happiness. There is much you can teach me, and I can find more honest ways of protecting you. It's time we started to trust each other again. I won't deceive you anymore and you can become open and vulnerable again, and we'll face the world together with renewed confidence and hope.'

On hearing this, deep down inside the Soul becomes happy. 'Soon they will remember me and start to communicate again. In coming together we will create such peace, love and happiness.' Quietly the Soul waits, knowing that without her the Heart will never heal permanently. She is patient, for the Soul knows that she must first rescue the Mind, which has become separated, lost, fearful and arrogant. 'Poor thing,' she thinks. 'Depending on yourself for so long, while I've been here all the time.'

reawakening innocence

*O*nce we were innocent; simple, pure and peaceful. We were ignorant of the body, knew nothing of mortality and had never experienced pain, disappointment or suffering. Before being born we existed as a soul without a body, never experiencing doubt or desire. Our soul entered this world in a pure and simple state, allowing us to be happy without reason. However, over time our happiness became conditional as the heart entangled itself in a world of attractions and relationships.

I remember watching two very young children playing together. When they finished their mothers asked them to hold hands on the way home. The little girl happily linked hands with the boy, whereupon he took her hand and threw her to the ground. She was unhurt but distraught from the shock. The boy's reaction had been unexpected. He was reprimanded as she was comforted. When they were ready to leave, the boy's mother told him to hold the little girl's hand again, properly. Innocently he held his hand out to her. But instead of taking it she stepped back, hiding her hands behind her back. Having experienced betrayal she was unwilling to trust him again and needed to protect herself. Having learnt to fear she was less innocent than before the incident. Though more experienced in life, she wouldn't be so unconditional and open with her trust. Her mind now contained a seed of doubt and uncertainty about others, and she needed to be defensive. She was less vulnerable but a tiny part of her inner beauty had been blemished.

Consider for a moment the many challenges we face in our lives. Although we have positive experiences of joy and happiness we have had many undermining encounters too. All of us go through different forms of physical, mental or emotional pain. When we consider how the little girl reacted, it is not difficult to understand how our original personality is modified by experience. As we gather layers of mistrust and defensiveness our innocence is lost or, more accurately, is obscured, becoming hidden more and more within our subconscious.

Yet we love our innocence. Special places, a scene in nature or the eyes of a child can reawaken innocence because they remind us of a time when we were peaceful and knew no conflict. When our innocence is reawakened we feel whole and yet what we are really experiencing is the essence of our spirit, untouched and serene. Enlightenment comes with the realisation that our peaceful, contented feelings of innocence are truly the silent, pure nature of our soul. This knowledge connects the heart and soul, giving us the courage to let go of the past and to trust in the future.

When we have learnt this we have begun to
understand that the power to heal is already
within us and all that remains is for us to
choose this.

ego

$\mathcal{T}$he Heart and Mind were talking. 'I can *feel*
something,' said the Heart. 'There's definitely
somebody else here.'

The Mind shivered. 'I can't see anyone, but I
feel it too and I don't like it.'

When the Heart and Mind start working
together, the Heart is the first to sense the Soul
emerging, because the Mind is reluctant to accept
what is now unfamiliar.

Recognising the opportunity, the Soul was
pleased. 'They can feel me again. It's been so
long.' With this she emerged from the shadows
of all their life experiences.

The Heart was engulfed by her love, while
the Mind became blissful and serene, and let go
of its fears and doubts. For a moment all three
became one, and all experienced the immense
power of love flowing through them like a

current. The Heart was utterly overwhelmed. The Mind recovered first. 'Who are you? Where did you come from?'

'I am your true self,' the Soul replied.

The Mind was not convinced but couldn't deny its experience. It had never been happier. 'How can you be my true self? I can feel you but not see you and that scares me. I don't remember ever knowing you before.'

'Once we were innocent of all of this,' the Soul said to the Heart and Mind. They immediately saw that she was talking about the body. 'At first we did not exist separately from one another. We were a pure being of light, love and peace. You were created so that we could experience life but then you forgot me and went out into the world alone.' The Heart and Mind felt guilty on hearing this.

'How could we have left you?' the Heart said.

'At first we belonged together but then the mind was attracted by the outside world,' replied the Soul. 'Someone gave him a name and he started to think of himself as a body. Then he convinced you to go with him. As soon as you left you lost the security of the love that we are and became dependent on others to feel loved, secure and happy.'

'So it's all my fault,' the Mind said.

'No,' the Soul replied, 'it's a natural process
and everyone does it. And anyway I came with you.'

Now the Mind was not convinced. 'Being with
you is a euphoric experience. How could you have
been here without us knowing it?'

'I changed my form. As you became body-
conscious you were deluded and developed a subtle
arrogance, believing you could manage alone. You
thought you could do anything and forgot about
me. But when you took the Heart with you, you
discovered you were vulnerable and that the
world was not so trustworthy. I went with you
but needed to develop another form for your
protection.'

'And?' prompted the Heart and Mind together.

'I entered your delusion and developed ego,
your false identity.'

When we adopt the body as our mistaken identity
we forget we are souls. We become separated from
everything and from everyone. Separation leads
to fear and ego is our solution. We develop ego to
secure our sense of identity and to stop us feeling

vulnerable. Ego gives us a sense of being who we
are based on our gender, colour, culture, religion,
profession, hobbies and interests. Everything that
can build or erode our self-esteem is included, as
are the self-doubts, desires and self-gratification
that accompany them.

When we choose inner-healing we rediscover
the love and peace of the soul and we begin to
remember the soul as our true identity. As we
reawaken innocence we let go of ego and become
soul-conscious. Each time we meditate it is as
though we invoke the soul, asking it to resurface
in our awareness. We begin to feel a sense of
unity and love. We begin to let go of the
deceptions of the body and body-consciousness,
and we find that the illusions ego creates simply
dissolve.

meditation

The meditation commentaries throughout this
book are designed as a healing journey to reunite
the heart, mind and soul, and to bring you a sense
of love and union. In my practice of Raja Yoga I
meditate with my eyes open. There are reasons for

this. Meditation is not meant to be an escape from reality or stress, it is meant to transform our way of experiencing life. In Raja Yoga, each time we meditate we are saying, 'I am a peaceful soul. This body is simply my vehicle or instrument.' We keep our eyes open during meditation because we are developing these ideas as a natural expression of our lives.

When we meditate we are not trying to stop the mind from thinking. We are trying to guide the mind by using positive thoughts about our virtues, our eternal identity or our relationship with God. Whatever we experience in life follows a pattern of thought. Stress, worry and depression begin with negative patterns of thinking. Peace and happiness begin with a positive thought. Meditation is about training the mind in right thinking, which leads us to experience deep peace, love or happiness. Listening to the commentaries on the companion CD helps to guide your thoughts towards the peace and serenity of your spiritual identity.

If you are not experienced with meditation it is helpful to do a relaxation exercise first. Sit in a comfortable, symmetrical position. Take a few deep breaths, then progressively relax your body from the feet upwards by contracting and relaxing

each muscle group in turn. That is, first the feet,
then the calves, then the thighs and so on.
Once your body is relaxed turn on the meditation
commentary. It is helpful to repeat the commentary
in your mind, rather than just listening to it.
This actively directs your thoughts and stops
your mind from drifting.

It is your choice whether to meditate with
your eyes open or closed. If you develop the
habit of open-eyed meditation you can use
meditation throughout your day. Whether in
meetings or during mundane activities you can
fill your mind with positive thoughts about your
eternal identity. Meditating in this way transforms
your nature and attitudes continuously. If you
have to close your eyes to experience the benefits
of meditation it is much more difficult. You
must set aside time, allow for privacy and are
unable to meditate automatically or in any
circumstances.

To practise open-eyed meditation rest your
eyes on a focal point of some sort, such as a
lighted candle, some flowers or an object or
picture that has spiritual significance. Don't
try to stare or concentrate on the object.
Simply be an observer then let the commentary
concentrate and direct your mind.

meditation commentary: spirit of innocence

I allow my body to relax. Breathing evenly and naturally, I turn my awareness inward. I find a silent space within, and I feel my own presence. I feel the pure energy of my own essence — just me — and for a few moments, untouched by the outside world, I am a pure, silent being. There is no one quite like me. I appreciate the special feeling that is me, and I appreciate my journey through life that has led me to the present.

I especially remember my early years — my spirit of innocence, my pure vision and trust. My natural spontaneity. And I recall my growth to adulthood. I recognise how my innocent spirit became overlaid by many fears, doubts, worries and troubles. But now, resting in the silent stillness of my being, I remember who I am. I go beneath the layers of fear and doubt and I again view myself and the world with innocence.

I create an image in my mind that expresses my innocence. Using my imagination I take my innocent spirit to a special place in nature. A place I have been before and where I appreciated the beauty of nature, or a special place that I will now create in my mind — perhaps a hidden valley full of wild flowers or a serene, peaceful place by the sea. I focus on the details of my special place. I notice the shapes, the colours, the fragrances. And with a child-like innocence, my spirit begins to dance naturally and joyfully, inspired by the beauty of my special place. My dancing spirit expresses my pure innocence and self-acceptance. Innocence moves me and I dance freely — feet gliding over the soft earth, a gentle breeze caressing my face and hair.

My dancing spirit returns to stillness and my eyes drink in the beauty of my special place. I absorb the peace and beauty of this place. It is my peace, my beauty. It is me. My spirit has once again awakened to its innocence.

a

being

of

love

unconditional love

One of my cancer patients recently died with complete acceptance. She was at peace with herself and her presence radiated love all around her. The spiritual state of acceptance is more than accepting death, it is a spiritual freedom that comes from letting go of ego and the consciousness of the body. Her soul was completely detached, unaffected and beyond fear. She stopped worrying, let go of her bodily concerns and became free.

Once released and free from the body, the soul simply *is*. With nothing to do or think about it becomes peaceful and its experience is one of love. As we go through a terminal illness we may suffer but it is only ego that dies — the brittle shell of false identities, illusions and conditioning. Stubbornly ego clings to the world it knows, until it cracks and breaks to yield new life, truth and understanding. Mental suffering is the result of fear, attachment and holding on when we have

lost control of our lives and circumstances.
If we can grasp this idea, we will never again
suffer the emotional trauma that comes from
resistance to change.

In the moment we finally let go, body-
consciousness and ego dissolve and we experience
freedom and unconditional love. Unconditional
love is the love of our soul. It brings a joyful
feeling of unity in which the boundaries that
separate us from nature, one another and God all
disappear. Unconditional love is a state of
surrender, not something we can control or direct.
It brings feelings of wellbeing and the wish to
benefit everyone. To give love unconditionally we
must become love. When we surrender to unconditional love we allow love to change and transform
our lives. Distinct from ordinary love, unconditional
love never creates dependence and is always free
from attachment. It is a state of being rather than
a need. It dissolves away impurities until we
experience only the real and divine.

Unconditional love removes sorrow from the
heart and leaves a clear impression of purity and
truth in the soul. It heals by extinguishing all
doubt about our immortality. When love achieves
less than this it is conditional, and this describes
most of the love we know.

becoming love

The Soul was smiling. She saw the confusion between the Heart and Mind, and looked on hopefully.

'You developed ego for our protection!' Heart and Mind exclaimed.

'Yes,' she agreed. 'For your protection.'

'But why? Why did you let us go through so much pain and suffering?' the Heart asked.

The Mind was perplexed. He was still in awe of the love that they had experienced. 'When you emerged it was as if we became one,' he protested. 'It felt as though we amalgamated in love, peace and unity.' The Soul beamed. They are getting close, she thought. 'I was exaggerating a little. We were never really apart. We all came under the spell of the body. I didn't mean to develop ego, it just happened that way. We forget who we are and where we come from but eventually we remember again. When we forget we separate.'

The Mind was relieved. 'So it wasn't my fault. It wasn't just me that wanted to make something of myself. But why did you let me take the blame?'

'Well, as I said, it happens naturally and no one is to blame. But I couldn't blame either of you

anyway,' the Soul said mysteriously. The Heart
asked why not. 'Because you belong to me,' the
Soul replied. 'And we belong to one another. When
we came under the spell of the body I too was
conditioned. Together we became conditional in
our love, trust and acceptance of others. We
developed many impressions of this world which
were distorted through the illusions of need, greed
and mortality. And we discovered something that
had never occurred to us before — fear.'

The heart and mind were spellbound by the
revelation that they were faculties through which
a soul thinks and feels. 'Our first mistake was
body-consciousness. We found fear and vulnerability
and our solution to fear was ego. Ego gave us a
feeling of strength and identity by separating our
experience from others. It gave us boundaries by
which we now define ourselves and look at others.
As we took on new roles and identities in life we
seemed to be expanding our experiences when, in
reality, we were limiting ourselves.'

'Although I've had many happy times I've been
hurt over and over,' said the Heart. 'Even after
experiencing your love, I'm afraid to let go because
I don't want to risk sorrow again. Yet deep down I
know I will have to separate from everyone I love
one day. What can we do?'

'We can heal together,' said the Soul. 'We can remember who we are and return to our original nature. We can return to love and recognise that we are eternal travellers.' Then addressing the Mind she said, 'You must have the thought, "I am a peaceful, all loving soul." While you,' she said to the Heart, 'must develop this as a feeling and have conviction in its truth. My role is to become it.'

Co-operating with one another through pure thoughts, pure feelings and pure being, they once again experienced peace and unity. All sense of separateness was healed as the Heart, Mind and Soul became unconditional love. They transformed to a very subtle and brilliant point of radiant light.

'Why can't we be like that all the time?' the Heart said, disappointed when the experience ended.

'That is our higher self,' replied the Soul. 'It was our original nature and form before we became body-conscious. When we become soul-conscious together we glimpse it again. To return to our original nature we must become soul-conscious all the time. But we have had many births, and body-consciousness is a deeply ingrained habit now.'

'What do I have to do?' asked the Heart.

'You must set yourself free,' replied the Soul. 'When nothing of the past remains to hurt you, you are free. You must let go of any bad things you have done or that have been done to you through forgiveness. Begin by forgiving yourself then forgive others, understanding that their actions were influenced by ego. They hurt you through fear and ignorance. When you forgive you release yourself from their continuing power over you. When you forgive you forget and the past is past. Not even memories remain to hurt you.'

'What shall I do?' asked the Mind.

'Set yourself free,' replied the Soul. 'Let go of fear and remember that everything is in divine order so you must trust and accept instead of passing judgement. Become a detached observer of the drama of life and understand that everything that happens is meant to be. Accept that there is a reason for everything, even if that reason is hidden from your sight. From now on, you must create beautiful relationships with your loving, peaceful thoughts.'

The Heart and Mind were mesmerised as she continued. 'When you do this together — forgive and forget, trust and accept — you are truly living in the moment and life is beautiful. Nothing of the past influences your feelings or actions, and nothing of the future causes you uncertainty or concern. Simply choose freedom by changing your ways.'

'What will you do?' they asked. Don't they realise I'm talking to myself? She smiled inwardly. 'I will experience God in a way that I haven't for thousands of years and when we do this we will be completely healed. Our original innocence will be renewed and we will be safe in the knowledge of who we are; protected by knowledge our innocence will be free of its original vulnerability. We will be confident and open. Our transformation and our pure love will change the world we live in.'

In an instant the Heart and Mind glimpsed the world returning to love. They experienced a moment of joyful union with like-minded souls, and in that moment love was revealed as an overwhelming power, everything it touched turned to gold. They realised that the journey to love was not just for themselves, it was for everyone. Love's mission is to heal the whole world.

meditation commentary: a being of love

I accept myself now. My past, my aspirations, my hopes, my dreams, my achievements and my mistakes all merge within the present moment.

I relax into who I am. I accept myself as I am.
I tune in to the silent stillness of my being and connect
with the original qualities of my spirit: gentleness ...
strength ... happiness. With gentleness I live a life of
love, not control — love. I have the strength to pursue
my own unique journey, to find truth and to live truth.
When I am at one with the love inside me, I experience
happiness.

In the pure simplicity of my spirit I find only love. Not
the desire to control or direct but real love. A love that
surrounds me in gentleness and acceptance, contentment
and humility. I am love. I allow the experience of love —
not seeking it externally but recognising it as part of my
inner nature. I feel the power of this love, uplifting me and
awakening my innate divinity. I become love.

I allow love to radiate through my spirit and reveal
itself in my thoughts, my words, my actions.

I observe without judgement and I reveal love.

I speak without arrogance and I teach love.

I act without complexity and I become love.

As I become love, I become divine. I am divine and
my life expresses the pure gentleness of my spirit. I feel
a deep sense of belonging to the world and the world
belonging to me. Through the power of my own divinity
I co-operate with love's task of revealing truth, creating
unity and healing the world.

healing

the

heart

the broken heart

*W*hen we suffer an inconsolable loss, when someone
we love dies or leaves us, we feel that our heart is
broken. Unless you have experienced the grief and
pain of such loss it is difficult to understand. We may
feel engulfed by a void of emptiness and despair,
completely helpless and out of control. Overwhelmed
by sorrow, hopelessness and desperation, our grief
expresses the separation from someone we love and
this can eventually help us heal and adjust to a world
without them. But why does our heart break? If love's
mission is to bring us happiness, healing and unity,
something else must have made us vulnerable.

Picture your heart for a moment. Better still,
draw it on a blank page. Now think about everyone
you love and everything that makes you happy,
including your interests and hobbies. Include the
things that make you feel safe and secure; your source
of income, your home and material things. Write or
draw each of these inside your heart. Spread them
out so they're not too close together. Now separate

the items by drawing lines around each. Your drawing illustrates how people and circumstances control our happiness. Our hearts depend on all these to remain contented. If you lose something important such as your home or job you become worried and unhappy. Our hearts are vulnerable to loss and change and we expend so much energy exercising control over the things that maintain our happiness.

Now empty the heart you've drawn of everything you put there and write just one word — *love*. Love is all the security you need, yet it seems elusive. By setting our heart on many things it is broken into many parts. As every relationship and all circumstances eventually change they only give the heart temporary happiness. Every relationship will end, and sorrow results from attachments that lead us to depend on others for happiness. It is attachment within love that makes us needy, and attachment that causes grief. Although we love the special people in our lives, our attachment to them makes us vulnerable to loss and separation.

So how do we love without becoming attached or dependent? When someone recovers from grief they have readjusted to life without the person they have lost. Full recovery from losing a partner is marked by our readiness to form a new relationship. When we fall in love again the cycle begins over as our happiness depends on someone new. While this is the normal cycle of our lives what we are really looking for is the love of our original innocence. Its love is dependable and cannot be stolen. Although this love lives deeply in our heart we forget its existence and substitute attachment to compensate for its 'loss'.

When we colour love with attachment we open our hearts in the wrong way, placing too many expectations and conditions on the people we love. We live with fear of loss and rejection. We demand a return for our love. If our love isn't received or reciprocated as we expect, we close our hearts and lock ourselves away. In time we can become disheartened and separated from love altogether, or we may give up, despair or feel stressed.

Attachment leads us to become broken hearted. We need to heal this habit of fear, body-consciousness and conditioning to find the love that is already within us.

healing a broken heart

We are responsible for our feelings. We can't blame anyone for how we feel because we decide how situations influence us. Healing is a choice, although you may never have thought it so. If you are angry, broken hearted or anxious it is time to choose differently. You are not your feelings — you may be experiencing anger, depression or fear but they are not *you*. They are acquired and once acquired they cloud your peace and inner beauty. Observe them and say, 'I am not angry, depressed or frightened. These are just feelings. It's time to let go of them and remember who I am.' But where did your feelings come from and how can you let them go?

The past has conditioned us, deceiving us into thinking we are mortal, vulnerable beings. We believe that we are born, we suffer and die. We think happiness is something to look for outside ourselves. We feel compelled to pursue our desires and protect our interests. With these thoughts we live in a present conditioned by the past, and project this conditioning onto an uncertain future. We doubt ourselves and doubt our fortune. All of these thoughts are mistakes; they create an illusion which separates us from the truth — that we are spiritual beings. This illusion is created by fear, which in turn comes from body-consciousness. The remedy to this illusion is the love that comes from the consciousness of our soul.

To let go of painful feelings we must do more than forgive or forget, as our pain can be triggered again by unkind words or attitudes. We need to erase these feelings from our subconscious to be secure in the future. Then we won't be vulnerable any more. To heal the heart we have to take our mind beyond our feelings and emotions, changing our awareness from one that is trapped by the body to one that is liberated and free. We may have to go through sorrow or grief before we have enough strength to move on, but eventually we must decide it is time to do so. Using our thoughts we can travel beyond our pain and discover the feelings and emotions of our inner truth, enabling us to look differently at our world.

In a recent meditation group I had been discussing how we can detach from our roles and the negativity of the world to enter the peace that lies within. I asked the group how differently we might look at the world if we were always peaceful in this way. A young man replied, 'More positively — we would stop looking at other people's weaknesses and understand that they want the same love and happiness as we do.'

With spiritual awareness we look beyond people's attitudes and behaviour with the realisation that they are no different from us. We stop judging others or looking at their weaknesses. Ask yourself, 'How can I recognise arrogance, greed or selfishness?' It must be that you have or once had these weaknesses too or how could you know what they are? If we examine the weaknesses of others we think about them, turn them over in our minds, talk about them and react against them. Every time we do this we surrender our own peace and react against our true self, and allow the negativity of others to influence and hurt us. If you ask yourself who controls the way you think and feel, you will see how you have handed that control to others. We often blame someone for hurting us or making us angry, but in reality we have chosen to be hurt or angry through our own faults, weaknesses or expectations.

Self-healing begins when we take responsibility for how we think, feel and experience life. Instead of looking at others we should look at ourselves, using the mind to recognise and cultivate our inner beauty and then face and transform our weaknesses.

To cultivate inner beauty you have to accept it then seek it. This is a challenge because it is difficult to know our own nature. Many of us are easily hurt by disparaging remarks, but we have trouble accepting the good qualities others see in us. In believing we have to be humble we don't accept our worth, and we must do this to see the value in others. Accepting your worth is the basis of true humility.

Acknowledging our inner beauty is challenging because we have cultivated the habit of looking at our defects. Imagine that your mind is a garden. When you look into it you see a bed of roses overgrown by weeds. You are tempted to remove these weeds — your weaknesses, bad habits and negative feelings — but this can be a thankless task. When we remove one weed another appears. If we relax our vigilance the garden becomes choked and overgrown again. First we need to develop and appreciate the beauty of our garden; the flowers of our pure qualities and virtues. There is a hidden sanctuary within every soul that is already perfect and complete with every God-given virtue. By journeying inwards you will find the key to your sanctuary and discover your original purity, innocence and happiness. This key is peace and the knowledge that you are a peaceful soul; it is the path to accepting your worthiness and your freedom.

We react to others' weaknesses because they are also our own. In the same way we can appreciate the beauty and qualities of others because these are already within us. You cannot admire someone else's serenity or generosity unless you actually possess and reawaken these qualities. Begin to heal your heart by appreciating your own beauty through others. What can you see that is pure and virtuous in those around you? As you honour their purity and virtues you are learning to love and respect yourself at the same time as giving love and respect. Look for virtues everywhere — tolerance, gentleness, openness, patience, mercy, generosity; think about them and reflect on them until their essence is felt in your heart, for their essence is love.

You must also discipline your mind so you don't see, reflect on, or speak of the defects and weaknesses of others. Simply tell yourself that this person has forgotten that they are a soul. Control your mind and if you have the wrong thoughts determine to stop them immediately. Avoid having negative feelings about anyone. Now you are co-operating with God's love and your heart is healing. You have recruited your mind for healing and you are healing more than past losses — you are returning to love. Soon pain, ego and attachment will simply disappear. As you return to love its power is released, removing your weaknesses and negativity.

letting go

*T*he Heart and Mind had already experienced extraordinary love and divine potential but still they couldn't let go. 'Why can't we surrender?' lamented the Heart.

'Because we have become addicted to and dependent on external supports over a long period of time,' replied the Soul. 'It's hard to let go of everything we have depended on for our love, security and happiness. You may feel guilty and defeated and think it's because you can't let go, but actually it's the other way round.'

The Mind grasped this very quickly. 'They're obstacles! Feeling guilty and defeated prevent us from letting go and surrendering.'

Confused, the Heart objected, 'But I'm feeling guilty *because* I haven't been able to surrender.'

'No, guilt and defeat are habits that arise from self-doubt,' the Soul explained. 'When we become disheartened we fall back on the support of our attachments or we give up altogether. When we experienced love together and glimpsed our divine potential, a window opened and revealed who we are. We were changed forever and there was no going back. But ego closed the window as quickly as it opened, making us wonder if it was just an illusion; telling us to depend only on what is real and true. What we experienced was real but ego plants the doubt that we can ever attain this, telling us to hold on to the world we know.'

The Heart and Mind were struggling to resolve this, so the Soul continued. 'Ego springs from fear and vulnerability, from loss of clarity and the illusions of a body-conscious world. To defeat ego we must become sure of our strengths, our opportunities, our creativity and ourselves. We must develop deep acceptance of ourselves, cast out doubt and dissolve our fear and uncertainties.' The Heart and Mind began to feel confident and hopeful again.

'If you simply try to become detached you will certainly fail. Life is sweet and you will feel too much loss.' The Soul seemed to address them now from a higher realm. 'Think of experiencing me as *I am* and you will realise you cannot fail. Success is guaranteed the moment you step away from illusion.'

The Heart was beginning to understand. 'By filling myself with truth I become honest and trustworthy, while the Mind develops clarity and understanding. Then there will be no foundation of self-doubt, guilt or the prospect of failure. To let go we have to keep our pure eternal form and original nature of innocence before us.'

'And stop feeling that we have failed when we act wrongly or lose sight of these,' added the Mind.

'Yes,' the Soul exclaimed. 'Be patient with yourselves. Remember me *as I am* to experience love, peace and happiness from within, and progressively let go your dependence on other things in a natural and easy surrender. The right understanding is that we are souls through which we see the true and the real; and the wrong understanding is that we are bodies through which we see a distorted illusion. As we let go we are freed from the need to control anything outside ourselves. When we are completely free we gracefully surrender to love's mission, and become messengers of peace to the world.'

meditation commentary: healing the heart

I allow my mind to settle into silence and peace. In this moment I put aside any unwanted thoughts and I focus my attention on the heart of my being. My heart is my silent secret place where I can feel life deeply as it is. In my heart I know intuitively what I want from life and

what I have to do to find it. In my heart I know myself
as a loving being, sure and kind, gentle and accepting.
But many times I have opened my heart in the wrong
way. I have opened my heart to love but put too many
expectations and conditions on that love. I demanded a
return for my love and when I didn't receive it I closed
my heart and locked myself away.

Yet the love in my heart is always there hidden and
waiting — like a tiny rose bud waiting for the right time
to bloom into a beautiful flowering rose. What do I need
for my love to emerge? Only to know that I am already
a being of love. I let go of the illusion that I have to draw
love into my heart from outside myself. As I sit here, as
I breathe, as I exist, I feel pure love in my heart. A love
untouched by time, space and conditions. It is as though
I am breathing in the fragrance and beauty of a perfect
rose and I hold this loving feeling gently within myself.
Within this love and beauty I feel a deep acceptance of
myself. My fears and uncertainties dissolve. I become sure
of myself in the drama of life — sure of my strengths,
sure of my opportunities and creativity, and sure of my
ability to overcome obstacles.

My heart is strong and able to hold on to love, and as
I give love and become loving — first towards myself and
then towards others — I attract love to myself. I become
like the fragrant rose, and I draw the love of others as they
come to appreciate my loving openness and beauty.

I open my heart completely to love. I cast out doubt and fear. I am a being of love, and I give my love freely and openly. My heart and the rose are one, offering my gentle fragrance without conditions and expectations. I am whole. I am complete. My heart is healed.

healing

your

soul

go beyond

One of my medical colleagues recently told me about her 'out-of-body' experience. As a child she was a passenger in a car that was involved in a serious head-on collision. Thrown free of the vehicle she lay unconscious and bleeding on the road. She recalls floating above the scene of the accident, watching her injured body being moved out of the way of oncoming traffic. She felt quite detached and peaceful, and recalled how her feelings and emotions were filled with clarity and insight. 'I felt at one with all of creation yet I was still clearly aware of who I was,' she said.

This is how I believe we experience death. As we leave the body, the soul moves beyond emotions and becomes a peaceful observer. Its separation from the realm of spirit is healed. And in that moment we have clarity and a preserved sense of identity. We experience unity and rediscover universal love. As we 'die', we heal; we move beyond physical, mental and emotional suffering. Two most significant aspects of separation are healed as we die. These are our separation from peace and from the unifying love of God. These two are a great loss to the soul, experienced after it surrenders its identity to the body and develops ego. When the soul heals it realises and experiences its true identity; ego is broken and truth revealed.

The soul's healing journey can begin in life if we listen to our spirit and go beyond our physical senses and emotions. Instead of being affected by the attitudes and negativity of others, we develop inner strength and power by turning our minds inwards and focusing on the awareness: 'I am a peaceful soul.' Rather than suppress or deny negative feelings I encourage you to develop this spiritual strength to help you deal with them. Many emotions simply merge within the realisation of truth, needing no other attention. Essentially, they are healed, but the difference between merging in truth rather than repressing in the subconscious is very subtle. When my colleague had her 'out-of-body' experience she witnessed her emotions in a clear and detached manner. She was able to do this because we are not our emotions and can be quite separate from them. Our emotions will only be healed when we recognise this.

empower your mind

𝒯o heal you must think of yourself as a spirit and rescue your mind from the negativity and conflict of the outside world. As a faculty of the soul, your mind can become a creative and valuable asset in your healing. When the mind is a faculty of the body its thinking is influenced by ego, reacting through negative emotions to what others say or do. Until you align your mind with your soul you don't have control over how you feel, but are at the mercy of other people or circumstances. We may begin the day feeling good, but one wrong word or some bad news can change all this. It is as though we have lost our self-respect and forgotten our immortality.

By aligning the mind with the soul we develop our mind's power. By power I mean a sense of strong self-determination and the capacity to think, feel and act in accordance with our highest principles. When we unite the mind with the soul our pure feelings of love and peace emerge, first in our thoughts, then in words and actions. The soul–mind connection results in positive feelings, creativity and actions based on love. When they arise from a foundation of love our thoughts are infused with the power to heal through our mind–body connection or through our relationships. In contrast, when the mind is disconnected from spirit it is trapped by ego with all its potential for fear and negativity, which adversely affects our health and relationships.

To develop the power of the mind we must pay attention to our thoughts and attitudes, putting a concerted effort into making these peaceful and pure-hearted. When we harness such thoughts we become conscious of the soul and break the ego of body-consciousness. I call this *surrender*.

Fear separates us from love and ego separates us from all that is divine. As we surrender our ego we become free from fear, allowing the pure, unconditional love of God to empower our souls. If you make the effort to remember that you are a soul, God helps and heals you. God reveals who you are, showing you that you are not separate from His love, and accepts you with complete forgiveness. Remembrance of God is ninety per cent of the effort required to free yourself from fear and ego. The other ten per cent addresses weaknesses and negativity through paying special attention to thoughts and actions that cause sorrow or distress. Anger, jealousy, excessive attachment, possessiveness and greed are features of ego responsible for the pain we experience.

In order to develop and concentrate the power of our thoughts and heal the soul, we must remain detached and disinterested in worldly matters beyond our control. We must try to bear responsibilities lightly and remain happy under all circumstances. Above all be sweet, humble and loving, and express truthfulness in your thoughts, words and deeds.

detachment

When Joanne was first told of her terminal cancer she suddenly felt as though she was in a dream. 'I could hear my doctor's voice but it was as though he was talking to someone else. I felt that I was observing the scene. I didn't feel upset. Actually, I was surprisingly relaxed but it just didn't feel like me.' For days afterwards she had 'this weird feeling that it wasn't real', and felt that she would wake up and realise she had dreamed the whole thing. In psychological terms this would be termed shock and denial, but I believe there is another explanation. A similar reaction can also occur during a life-threatening accident or following serious trauma. We become detached observers, and don't feel the emotional or physical pain we should be experiencing. During the shock our consciousness shifts from the body to the soul and protects us from what is happening. In an accident the soul is also preparing to leave the body should this be necessary.

When we adopt the attitudes and awareness of the soul we become detached from the body yet remain easy, natural and loving. Detachment is healthy for the soul. We calm down and become observers, watching the scenes of our lives, drawing wisdom from them and increasing our understanding. Through detachment we concentrate the power of truth, first in our soul and later in our words and deeds. Detachment gives us the power to withdraw, to remain peaceful and to develop tolerance, acceptance and understanding. Detachment is about truth, not about distancing ourselves from others. It allows us to relate to each other through our highest values. Detachment enables you to rise above the negativity and violence of the world, to remain peaceful under all circumstances and to bring peace of mind to others.

When we are peaceful we don't worry. Whatever is happening is temporary so if someone is suffering we understand that they are moving through pain. If you understand the temporary nature of all things you can comfort others in pain, be close to them, listen to them, understand them and extend your love and compassion without feeling sorrow. When you can detach yourself from the deception that death is the end of life or that suffering can ruin life, your spiritual knowledge has practical expression — it brings comfort and hope.

Detachment concentrates the power of peace in your soul, allowing the pure feelings of your spirit to become creative thoughts that reach others. In meditation or prayer you can send healing thoughts to the world, to particular places or to individuals you wish to support from afar. In your home or at work you can create a peaceful and healing atmosphere to benefit others without them knowing. In time, you may develop a healthy disinterest in worldly matters while feeling a deep compassion for all beings. Such compassion is stable and is not altered by external events because we have detached ourselves from the illusion of mortality and the deception of ego. When we are detached from the negativity of our worldly relationships we feel at one with our human family. In truth, we detach only from that which is not real or eternal, which gives us the vision to see only spirit and extend only love.

humility and self-respect

One of the concerns my patients frequently
express about dying is the fear that they will
lose their dignity. Jenny was just thirty-seven and
suffering from advanced breast cancer when she
expressed this fear to me quite poignantly. 'It's
not dying I'm afraid of; it's the process — what I
have to go through. I hate the thought of becoming
dependent, of losing control of my mind and bodily
functions. If I have to die I want to do so with
dignity,' she told me.

Jenny did become dependent. She did occasionally lose control of her bodily functions, but she did
die with dignity. She learnt peaceful acceptance, let
go of her fears and had the *inner dignity* that comes
with self-respect. She brought peace and acceptance
to her family while they cared for her at home.

Jenny's fears were the concerns of the body
and the ego, but her dignity was that of spirit,
although she had no particular spiritual beliefs.
Once she accepted that she wasn't the person she
used to be and could no longer do the things she
was used to doing, she yielded. She let go of her
need for independence and control and allowed
her family to care for her. 'It was an amazing

transformation,' her mother told me. 'From being frightened, angry and depressed Jenny became easy-going and contented — a joy to be with. She seemed to know that everything would be all right and had an amazing strength that supported everyone.'

Inner dignity — the dignity of the soul — comes from self-respect. Self-esteem relates to our appearance or achievements while self-respect comes from the experience of our spirit, its radiance and beauty. When we come to know our spirit, truth is awakened in our hearts and we begin to understand everything we see. We master our feelings and emotions, acquiring inner power without any wish to control others. A natural thought emerges: 'I am complete and whole, and worthy of God's love.' This is self-respect. It allows us to feel secure. We no longer need anything from others, and aren't affected by their unkind words or actions. If we lack self-respect, we react with anger or hurt when someone criticises us. On the other hand, if we have spiritual knowledge and know the value and beauty of our soul, we have the self-confidence to remain peaceful and unaffected.

Self-respect broadens our perspective and brings us freedom. A feeling of self-worth free from arrogance or ego accompanies our recognition of the soul. Recognising the soul is humbling; finding our 'truth' allows us to see the value of all souls. Valuing others through valuing yourself is the meaning of real humility which is expressed through a gentle and benevolent nature. Humility and self-respect protect you from feeling insulted and jealous. They stop you from being judgemental and make you strong. Humility is the virtue that tunes your heart to God's purity and power. It renews the soul's divinity, giving it the freedom to serve humanity with utmost simplicity. Through humility and self-respect your soul is healed as the illusion of separation from divine love is removed.

freedom from illusion

The Heart and Mind were mesmerised. A very beautiful figure was dancing nearby, her every movement sensual and sublime. One moment she seemed unaware of their existence but then she would smile at them, lifting a veil over her face to reveal her eyes. Such beautiful eyes. As though enchanted, the Heart and Mind were drawn towards her. She began to leave, one finger beckoning them to follow. Dancing and laughing, she led them across fields and valleys to the cities and the bright lights.

She gave them rest and comfort and granted them imaginary pleasures. But when the Heart and Mind tried to get closer to her, she slipped away, taking them with her on a worldly dance. She made them happy and they indulged themselves in her beauty, as she fulfilled their desires. And when for a moment she disappeared, they searched frantically until they found her sitting by a stream, waiting. Above the veil, her eyes were full of mischief. She allowed them to approach.

The Heart and Mind felt the thrill of anticipation and excitement as they walked towards her and together slipped the veil from her face. The sight made them recoil in revulsion. Sick with fear, the Heart and Mind cowered as she adopted a monstrous and fearsome form. The pleasant scenes were replaced by a violent storm, and the Heart and Mind knew they were going to die. Having completely trapped the Heart and Mind she was triumphant, but suddenly sensing something she screamed in anger. Her form alternated between mesmerising beauty and repulsion. Then she was gone. The peaceful scenes returned as, shaken and terrified, the Heart and Mind saw the Soul smiling down at them.

'What a mess you two are in,' the Soul chuckled.

The Heart trembled. The Mind spoke first. 'What was that?' he stammered.

Still smiling, the Soul looked at them both. 'It's safe now,' she said gently. 'She's gone. Well, for the time being at least.'

In the presence of the Soul, the Heart and Mind were comforted. They absorbed her strength and peace. 'Who was she?' asked the Heart.

'She *is* Maya,' the Soul replied. 'She adopts many forms and deceives with her illusions. Maya has been with you all along but you can't recognise her until you remember me. Now she doesn't want to let you go, and she will do everything in her power to keep you attracted to the old world.'

'Where does she come from?' the Mind asked.

'Maya means illusion,' the Soul replied. 'She is your creation. When you forget me you forget who you are. As you adopt the body and develop the identities of ego, Maya becomes your companion. In her sweetest form she leads you to gratify worldly needs. Her repulsive face is a projection of your vices: greed, anger, jealousy, arrogance and lust. Through your attraction to Maya you develop a judgemental attitude and the capacity for evil. Even in her sweetest form she deceives you because she pulls you away from truth.'

'But why didn't we know she was with us?' the Heart asked.

'When you forgot me,' the Soul replied, 'she

became the truth. She didn't have to catch your attention because you learnt to see through her eyes, listen with her ears and think with her mind. Maya is a projection of ego's control over you. The world today is Maya's kingdom. She traps the heart and mind in her illusion and battles against truth.'

'So Maya is our normal state of being until we begin to realise our spiritual identity,' the Mind said.

'Yes, and when *we* realise our spiritual identity we begin to recognise her games. We come to know her as she is and begin the battle to break her hold over us, rejecting her deceptions in an effort to see the truth. Maya is angry when we invite God back into our lives because she loses her power. Having trapped us in her web for so long she is very powerful and doesn't let go without a fight. This is why the spiritual path can be a struggle, and why so many become disheartened and give up.'

'How can we become free?' the Heart and Mind asked together.

'Take up her challenge!' the Soul exclaimed. 'The battle against Maya begins by recognising all her forms. Make yourselves strong by remembering your eternal form and transform your weaknesses. Maya will die, but the closer you come to God the harder she will try to make you fall back on your old ways. This is an unseen battle in which you become courageous warriors who free the world from her influence.'

The Heart and Mind were inspired, as the Soul joined with them and they felt the sweetness of union with all life. As the three of them separated, a shadowy figure with a face of timeless wisdom appeared before them. 'Who are you?' asked the Heart and the Mind.

'I am your intellect. You haven't used me in a long time. I discern truth from illusion and keep you in spiritual awareness to enable you to reject Maya. While you have been ruled by ego you have only seen falsehood. But once you recognise Maya you find me too. Now you must use me to set yourselves free.'

The Heart and Mind knew the Intellect was an old friend, and they rejoiced in the hope of freedom.

meditation commentary: healing the soul

I allow my body to rest. I take a deep breath in, and as I breathe out I release any tightness or tension that I am holding in my body. I am becoming loose and free and relaxed.

I allow my thoughts to settle as I prepare to meditate. I let my mind rest. I absorb the music into my soul. I listen to the gentle sounds and I follow the sequence of notes as the music soothes my mind. I absorb the music and I relax completely.

Above me I perceive a shining star — a star radiating infinite light from a central point. I am moved by the star's perfect beauty. The star's light is drawing me like a magnet and I feel my spirit rising. Breaking free from my bodily restrictions, my spirit flies upwards towards the star. I am floating in the freedom of endless space. The star attracts me closer to itself. I am drawn even closer until I am right by the heart of the star.

I am surrounded by a soft silvery glow. I sense that this light has a living warmth which enters my spirit. I know this star is a gift from God, and through this star God is caressing my spirit with light and love. Within this light and love my spirit rests peacefully. I am peaceful. I am content. My spirit is whole. My spirit is healed through God's love and peace.

As I absorb divine love, the light of God reaches every aspect of my spirit. I allow God's loving light into every dark corner. The light touches my fear. I feel the fear dissolve into a loving light of acceptance. I absorb loving divine light into my dark moods of anger and I feel a growing easiness and tolerance in my spirit. The light touches my worry and I let go of my concerns for the future. I let go of what happened in the past and I

become peaceful and carefree. Every aspect of my spirit
is light and free. I have absorbed light and peace deeply
into my spirit and I radiate this light and peace outwards.
I rest awhile in the gentle, loving light of God.

healing

through

love

and

divinity

surrender

When I first met Paula she had advanced cancer of the bowel. Before her illness she had been an influential high-achieving professional, but realising the disease was progressing she was reassessing her life. She described herself as a 'doer' who had always put others first. Despite her success she had a nagging feeling of inadequacy and was always very self-critical. She had fought her cancer in much the same way. Determined to beat the odds, she had tried complementary therapies, prayer and meditation. However, the disease got worse and the weakness and pain she experienced eroded all her hopes and her resolve to beat cancer.

She confided her feelings to me. 'Like everything else in my life, I've been doing everything because I thought I had to. I've been doing meditation and doing complementary medicine. Frankly, I'm sick of it. What I really want is to love myself, to trust and surrender, and experience God loving me.' I asked

Paula how she saw God and His role in her life.
She said, 'I believe God is all that is good within
us and all that is divine outside us. If I could
trust in this belief and willingly surrender, I would
experience so much divine love. Despite the faith
I have had since a child, I have never felt as close
to God as I do now. All this time my busy life,
my activities and my pride in achievements have
been separating me from the oneness that I now
experience with God.'

Paula had recognised that the divine is ever-
present, and that our thoughts and actions either
separate or unite us with God. Surrender is the way
we heal our separation. Through the experience
of God's love we begin to let go of our ego, our
worldly desires, our doubts and our painful past.
As we surrender and let go, the illusions we
have created dissolve and we find truth. We
understand who we are and why we are here.
Division and conflict disappear from our lives
to be replaced by understanding, tolerance
and acceptance.

When we surrender ego we accept God's love
and power instead of relying on our own. God's
love becomes our own and makes us feel we belong.
This experience of love is so perfect that the past is
erased from our minds. Suffering and pain vanish

and are transformed into feelings of gratitude as our eternal form becomes clear.

It is easy to surrender. You can surrender by going to a peaceful place or by sitting in a room with some gentle music playing. Once settled, remember, it is only an illusion that we are separated from God. To surrender your ego and free yourself from illusion, meditate on and repeat the following affirmations slowly:

'I let go of my body.' (Feel that your body is entrusted to you by God.)

'I let go of my roles.' (Believe that the things you do are entrusted to you by God.)

'I let go of my relationships.' (Affirm that all the people in your life are God's children.)

'I let go of this world.' (Embrace the belief that healing the world is God's responsibility.)

'I let go of desires and belong to You.' (Feel God's companionship.)

'I allow Your love to reach my soul.' (Experience God's heart touching your own.)

'I accept You completely.' (Accept God in your life.)

'I am a child, Your loving child.' (Know God as a loving parent who belongs to you.)

'There is only You and I.' (Feel your union with God.)

Surrender brings us into a full relationship

with God, and we experience our eternal form
through the power of God's love. Practise this
surrender to experience the power of belonging
and you will experience the healing of divine
union.

the intellect

*E*xperiencing surrender is wonderful but
maintaining the experience is challenging. We
discern our lower self from our higher self by
finding God and recognising ourselves as souls.
Our lower self is expressed through the mind as
body-consciousness governed by ego, whereas our
higher self finds expression when we are governed
by spiritual knowledge. The lower self creates an
illusion, or Maya, when it separates from divinity
and looks at the world through its own arrogance.
This conditions everything we see. It is only when
we experience truth that we awaken to challenge
our own creation. The problem we face is that
the soul has become too weak through too much
comfort, or through despair or anger about things
that go wrong.

There are three aspects of illusion that separate

us from spiritual healing and fulfilling our highest
potential. These are allowing yourself to be
influenced or controlled by others, and having
attachment to people or things. The haphazard
influences of others prevent the recognition and
experience of our true self, making it difficult for
us to remain close to God. When we allow ourselves
to be controlled we cut off our uniqueness and lose
our freedom to express spiritual values. Through
attachment we become dependent on others for our
state of wellbeing or look for support in external
things. We are deceived and don't think about
developing who we are to our fullest potential.
These three aspects of illusion are created through
the eyes of ego, and are reflections of fear. Maya
adopts these forms to keep us separated from the
divine nature of our souls and God. She makes us
believe that what ego sees is real.

Spiritual knowledge loosens Maya's grip on us
and we discover there is a choice between truth
and illusion. We can choose to be masters of
ourselves; creators of our destiny. The choice is
made through the intellect, which discerns truth
from illusion, recognises Maya's many forms, and
guides us towards acts of purity and virtue. After
being overshadowed by Maya, the intellect can
begin to develop judgement and decision-making

powers. This requires some introspection and a relationship with God, which gives strength and sustenance to the soul.

Through the intellect the sorrow in our hearts is healed by the light of true understanding. We learn how to receive God's love and how to allow this love to reach others. The intellect disciplines the mind, identifying negative thoughts and feelings, and frees us. Our intellect identifies the love and peace of our soul and we stop acting in ways that hurt ourselves or cause others pain.

The intellect relies on a balance of reflection and experience. Too much thinking gives you a headache, yet understanding grounds experience and provides stability. By surrendering ego you activate the divine intellect; illusion is challenged and you become a child of God.

healing through Raja Yoga (divine union)

My spiritual journey began in 1984 at a life–death transitional workshop with Elisabeth Kübler-Ross. The workshop was designed as a cathartic experience

to encourage the expression of deeply repressed
pain from the past. I relived the childhood loss of
my baby sister's cot-death and broke down completely.
Then a remarkable thing happened. I was filled
with love and a blissful sense of unity in which I
felt at one with all. The happiest sensation of my
life followed immediately upon the release of my
deepest sorrow. I had no feeling of being separate
from anything or anyone and no awareness of my
physical body, yet I retained a sense of self. It was
a feeling of complete unity in which I retained my
identity. I now understand that this was a yoga
experience.

Releasing grief had opened a window to my soul.
Looking inward through this window I experienced
the love, peace and purity of my original innocence.
Outwardly I was immersed in the unifying power of
God's love. I now understand that this experience
of God was intimately connected to recognising
myself as a soul.

My experience in Elisabeth Kübler-Ross's
workshop was intensely motivating. I was convinced
that I had experienced God and I tried daily to
have direct union with God through meditation.
Sitting on an escarpment near my home I made
intense efforts every morning, without success.
Then one day I had the thought that God might

be trying to reach me. Instead of making so
much effort I simply opened myself up, let go
and created a sense of allowing God to reach me.
I was immediately uplifted with feelings of pure
love and unity: the same feelings I had experienced
at the workshop, but there was a new emotion, a
feeling of deep compassion for humanity. I had
stumbled on this divine union at the workshop,
but now I discovered that it was available to me
through meditation. This was my first experience
of Raja Yoga, although it was another eight years
before I encountered the Brahma Kumaris World
Spiritual University and their teachings on this
discipline. (The literal meaning of yoga is union,
while Raja means king. Raja Yoga means to have
union with the Supreme soul or union with God
(divine union). Simply put, it is a way of constantly
remembering God.)

In the last sixteen years I have learnt that the
only thing we need to heal is the illusion of separateness. By remembering that I am a soul, I recall
the Supreme and experience the healing power of
love and unity. When I forget this truth I separate
myself from the intrinsic peace of my soul and
the love of God. We are separated from love when
we are body-conscious and influenced by ego. We
are separated from love when we have negative

thoughts and feelings. We are separated from
love when we form opinions and develop attitudes
about others or when greed drives us to satisfy
our desires. When we see others as different we
are separated from love. Every separation from
love is a separation from truth. When we are
honest and true, God's love finds us and heals us.
When you see others as children of God you know
them as your brothers and sisters. If you have
respect for others and stop judging them you
become humble. If you stop thinking about right
and wrong God takes you into His heart and
makes you an instrument of love.

The healing of Raja Yoga or divine union
makes the soul visible so that others can recognise
and transform themselves. When we project our
body-consciousness and ego we see a competitive
world full of differences. This shadow of Maya is
our own projection. It creates an illusion that hides
the soul. When we are being true to ourselves and
we accept divine healing, truth and unity are
visible in our words and actions. If we also let go
of the desire for recognition we free ourselves of
ego and become instruments of divine influence.

When I experienced this healing I felt at one
with all, yet I retained my sense of identity. I was
immersed in the experience of God and understood

that this was God and not just myself. To know
God requires subtle recognition. Raja Yoga teaches
us that we souls are infinitely tiny points of living
energy and that God, the Supreme Soul, is a loving,
pure and powerful resident of the incorporeal
dimension. This knowledge allows us to find God
in the non-physical world and to experience union
with His most powerful form. The Supreme Soul
purifies the deepest aspects of our souls, liberates
us from our past actions and recreates us in His
image. When we heal our illusion of separation we
experience more than the divine love of God; we
adopt the nature and form of that love.

union

'*T*o experience union with God only co-operate
with truth,' the Intellect said to the Heart and the
Mind. 'Truthful thoughts transform all actions into
expressions of love.' With this the Mind and the
Intellect merged into one, bringing feelings of
supreme power and control, understanding and
acceptance. The Heart followed uniting with the
Mind and the Intellect until they became indivisible
pure energy. Rising from the physical plane they

entered a subtle realm of light and knew they
were free. The Soul was blissful. Her faculties had
returned. From within her the Intellect was quietly
content, having silenced the Mind's constant
chatter and the Heart's grievances. Their union
was ecstatic.

They were seated in the very heart of God
experiencing divine love. They saw infinite light
and knew it was their own, merged in God's
infinite nature. They felt drawn, pulled by an
invisible magnet towards the source of God. As
they reached the source, the origin, they found
that they were looking in a mirror. 'In My
likeness you become truth and we are one,' the
voice of God was one of silent understanding.
'To know Me, know yourself and return to Me.
Fix your mind on Me and have merciful feelings
for those who have forgotten everything.' With
these words, worldly scenes and images were
placed before them, alternating from violence
and terror to self-indulgence and glee. 'Nothing
is right or wrong in the world you see. It simply *is*.
When you know Me and understand this you are
co-operating with the power of love. Transforming
yourself with love, you are taken into My heart, and
I work through you to light the lamp of awareness
in hearts and souls throughout the world.'

A new scene appeared before them. They saw a perfect world of breathtaking beauty where peace and happiness reigned in the hearts and minds of humankind. A world where nature was in complete harmony. Cruelty, conflict and sickness didn't exist. The Heart, the Mind and the Soul saw that this was a new world with divine order.

'This is your creation!' they exclaimed.

'No, it is ours,' God replied. 'I can do nothing without those who recognise Me. But first you …' At that moment the Mind wondered whether this vision was true. Suddenly they experienced a sensation of falling and in a moment they were sitting opposite the triumphantly grinning Maya. The Soul realised her mistake. She had allowed Maya to place a doubt in her mind and this one thought removed her from the truth. The Soul gathered herself with pure thoughts of her eternal identity and the final words of divine love returned. 'But first you must be victorious over Maya and belong only to Me.' The Soul used her Intellect, Heart and Mind to challenge Maya.

'I have seen and recognised the truth. I know myself as I am. I am healed and can remove your shadow from this world.'

With this, Maya disappeared.

meditation commentary: divine healing

$\mathcal{I}$ imagine myself in a place of natural beauty. My spirit resonates with the beauty around me and reminds me of my own beauty and gentleness. I feel the peace of this place, and my spirit basks in the simple beauty of this peace. I enjoy the silent space around me, and my mind rests peacefully in the silence.

As my spirit becomes free from worldly connections I open myself to the awareness of the divine. I connect with the divine in my own way. I am silent and still before God. I surrender my spirit to the divine. I let God love me. I absorb the eternal beauty and love of God within my heart. I am worthy of this love. God knows me, understands me and loves me with unconditional love. God looks upon me with love only. God knows the beginning, the middle and the end of me. I accept God's divine love and together we become love. I am a child of love. I belong to the divine. I rest in the stillness of God's love and I am bathed in peace and loving acceptance. With this love I experience pure contentment. I release the pain of unsatisfied desires and complicated relationships and I surrender to the beauty of God's loving acceptance of me.

Together, combined in love, we radiate love to the

people in my life. I send out heartfelt feelings of loving acceptance and appreciation to my family, to my friends, to my colleagues. I reach out to their hearts with pure love. I send them God's gift of pure love and support. My heart is overflowing with love.

healing

our

world

becoming a world-server

*H*ealing ourselves is the path to truth and unity. Only body-consciousness stands in the way of world peace. Remove body-consciousness and happiness and abundance will, I believe, return to our planet.

When I first began to meditate I used to sit on an escarpment overlooking the sea and a rainforest near my home. Through meditation it was easy for me to feel close to God, and I became absorbed in a contemplative experience that was almost visionary. I saw images of a chaotic world in transformation. I saw enlightened people around the world becoming soul-conscious. They emerged from the ruins of a civilisation that had lost its moral values and could no longer solve its problems or conflicts. They came from all walks of life and shared a common goal of awakening others to this unique age.

Connected by common thought and purpose, these souls form a network around our globe. Although they barely know each other or fully comprehend their purpose, they are making a joint spiritual effort to free other hearts and minds from the deceptions of body-consciousness.

I saw these souls returning to God. Each engaged in healing his or her separation from God, and forming a deep and powerful union with God. Through divine love they became instruments for a shift in awareness through which all souls are healed and liberated from body-consciousness, ego and illusion. I saw a community emerging where everyone lived peaceful, harmonious and happy lives. If this sounds familiar, you may be one of those souls. If so your task is to heal and transform yourself, and reveal truth to the world. You can become an example of truth and of peaceful living within your community. Seek out others like yourself to meditate together and strengthen the unity of your connection with the divine.

I believe that with true healing, our hearts, minds and spirits turn towards the world, serving others through acceptance, love and understanding. We are no longer afraid of death and are never disillusioned. We have a deep awareness that healing is a potential we all have, and faith that healing is inevitable. True healing gives us self-respect through the knowledge and experience

of our soul. We become steadfast and unshakeable
no matter what circumstances or events we face in
life, and we have merciful feelings towards souls
that have forgotten their true identity. To become
a world-server we must accept divine love and
reveal it to the world.

understanding the drama: it's all good

*R*aja Yoga has taught me to see that everything
is ordered and predestined — a 'drama' being
enacted on the world stage. This requires me to
be non-judgemental and to see that every soul is
playing his or her own unique role. Understanding
this drama is essential to living in peace and
remaining beyond the influence of negativity.

The cycles of life present challenges to our
spiritual endeavour. Accepting change as part
of the ebb and flow of life or considering that
everything is part of God's plan are common ways
of approaching life, but they don't provide long-
term answers. We can remain relaxed and laid
back when things are easy, but can also become
lazy in our spiritual effort and fail to develop

serenity and wisdom. Then when problems arise
we struggle. Deep down we don't really believe that
God's plan includes conflict, suffering or abuse, and
when we see things that make our faith waiver we
become disillusioned and angry.

Many of the natural rhythms of life are cyclical,
such as the changing seasons, the timeless decay
and renewal of nature, the cycle of birth and death
and the loss and renewal of our divinity. Eternal
life is, I believe, spirit rising and falling from
innocence through body-consciousness and back
again. In Raja Yoga we are taught that human
souls leave God and go through a cycle of successive
births, collecting impressions of past actions,
relationships and circumstances. As we journey
through these successive lives, body-consciousness
increases and the soul's original purity and power
is dispelled. The ego is substituted for purity and
we turn to vices for protection, temporary gain
and self-gratification. The accounts of our actions
go with us into each new birth, bringing fortune
and misfortune.

In this cycle we move from Utopia, the
'Golden Age', to a community that is chaotic
and disordered — the present 'Iron Age'. Souls
who are born later in the cycle join the first-born
souls on the world stage. The world population

increases until all souls occupy physical bodies.
By the end of the Iron Age everyone is body-
conscious, having accumulated the karma[1] of
past actions. These karmic accounts include those
requiring personal settlement, those that emerge
as relationship problems and those that belong to
groups and communities. Consequently the world
population is gripped by disease, premature death,
conflict and war. The ecological order is seriously
disrupted, leading to global crisis, political
upheavals and natural disasters. But throughout
history one soul remains that never enters the
cycle of birth and death. This ever-pure soul is
the one we call God. In Raja Yoga, we see God
as the living 'seed', a point of light that contains
all knowledge of the soul, of religions and of our
world. In answer to our plight, to our negativity,
suffering and need, God plays His role as a purifier
and world transformer.

For world transformation, for peace and purity to
re-emerge, humanity must settle its karmic accounts.
We must tolerate scenes of chaos, deprivation and

---

[1] Karma is a Hindi word meaning action. Karmic accounts are
the accumulated influence of past actions on the soul. The
settlement of negative accounts from wrong action has a
cleansing effect, but can involve suffering and difficulties.

victimisation. Everything we see has a hidden foundation. Through settlement of their karmic accounts, souls become healed, free and pure; ready to return to the heart of God. Raja Yoga teaches us that we live in an age where the world is undergoing an essential cleansing of all that separates us from divine love.

A sense of destiny, the belief in spirituality and the philosophy of karma help us to heal ourselves and the world. But to heal and to serve others we must be stable and unshakeable in our beliefs. When we have a framework through which to view the world, we can detach ourselves from the distress and difficulties others around us are experiencing. We can see how their troubles have arisen from the past and that the settlement of this karma is ultimately good. Instead of being affected by shocking headlines, we can keep our hearts and minds free, and be merciful and loving towards all souls. This type of detachment draws us closer to being part of a spiritual solution to the world's suffering. It is a way of giving, a way of loving. If we see all souls as playing out their roles we stop judging others and accept them with ease. With this strong sense of self-love, respect and power fill our lives and help us to fulfil the needs of others.

By understanding that the chaos in the world
today is an essential aspect of change we begin to
recognise that God's love is with us. Instead of
struggling with the world we seize opportunities.
God's task is to attract, inspire and teach souls
to become the instruments through which He
works. Our destiny is intimately linked with world
transformation, and our own healing is connected
with the healing of others. God teaches us this
intimacy and love's mission carries this message
to the world.

healing thoughts

*H*ealing the world involves the spirituality
of pure thoughts that renew unity, peace and
happiness. Our thoughts are extended beyond
ourselves and sent out as vibrations. Inwardly
these are mood states, while outside ourselves they
create an atmosphere. One person can change the
atmosphere in a room or among a group of people
through his or her mood and quality of thought.
When a group shares a common thought the
atmosphere carries the power and purpose of that
thought, which influences the outcome of their
desire. For instance, we are all familiar with the

beneficial effect of a home crowd on the performance of sports teams.

I have the conviction that when we meditate our thoughts and peaceful vibrations benefit thousands of souls separated by distance. If our meditation is concentrated we can extend our own healing to the world. Through meditation we grow spiritually and come to realise that no one's healing is complete until everyone becomes whole, because we are all spiritually connected. We must see everyone's suffering as our own and understand that we won't be free until everyone is liberated from body-consciousness. Unless I heal myself I cannot heal the world, and unless I heal the world I cannot heal myself. We need to develop a common unifying thought for world healing, self-realisation and a community that follows the highest values of living.

To connect our thoughts with those who are suffering requires us to understand that they have separated from truth and that they are still suffering the karma of this separation. This is merciful vision. Merciful vision also projects our understanding that we are souls. It helps us to accept and forgive the wrong actions of others in the knowledge that they are influenced by mistaken beliefs. Rather than focusing on each person, we use merciful vision to channel the atmosphere of

divine love into the world. Become soul-conscious
and feel merciful towards those who have lost their
love for truth — only time separates them from
enlightenment. Unless we co-operate to bring the
time of their healing closer, our own healing will
be delayed.

Don't carry worries with you; simply think,
'Drama, sweet drama!' Be content and let
nothing disturb you. Give good thoughts to
others and understand that these healing
vibrations are the benevolence of a charitable
soul. Don't send worry, anxiety, doubt or anger
into the atmosphere. Give loving feelings to the
world throughout your day and through these
feelings you will be connected to all souls. Remain
happy and sustain your own spiritual energy to
serve others. In time the power of unified thought
will create world peace. Simply accept this and
make it your life's purpose.

be an angel

*T*raditionally, angels are depicted with wings,
have a benevolent nature and are messengers of
God. As we heal, our separation from God's love
and form dissolves away and we experience a

transformation. The influence of our past experiences and our vices are removed from our souls. We remember who we are spiritually and our original nature of purity, peace and innocence is revealed once again. We begin to experience divine union and become world-servers. Our self-respect dissolves ego, spiritual feelings replace those of body-consciousness and we develop the capacity to fly on wings of benevolent thoughts. In Raja Yoga this is the angelic stage of spiritual development. It is a human potential and its attainment helps to heal the world we live in.

I remember one of my patients having an experience of the angelic stage as he lay dying. His name was Ralph. He had attained peace and was going to leave his body within a few days. I asked him how he was feeling and his response was unique. 'I feel like I'm blessing everyone,' he told me, 'I'm incredibly light, almost floating. It feels as though I am surrounded in light, as though there is a huge cocoon or halo around me. At times I can see it. I lie here feeling as though I'm rising from my body and just keep seeing light all around me. Sometimes I feel that I am part of it.' As he told me this, I began to experience the things he described and I suddenly understood what he meant by 'blessing everyone'.

Ralph continued. 'Although I'm lying here I don't feel limited to my body. If I think of anyone, past or present, it feels as though I'm instantly with that person and that my presence is a blessing. It seems that my mind can be extended beyond this body, and it feels as though I'm travelling in the light I was describing.' After searching for the right words, he told me one final truth: 'There is nothing but love, inside and out. I have become love.'

When people enter a state of acceptance before they die, their spirit has let go of ego and barely holds on to the body. Only the body and ego die while the soul is liberated and free to enter the dimension of light, so death is a time of healing. At the time of death our ethereal (light) body separates from the physical. The soul, taking its impressions from this and previous lives, travels on to be reborn.

Similar to the dying process, but through free will, we become angels when we let go of the body as identity, free ourselves from ego and liberate ourselves from the illusion. To be an angel, remember divine love, heal yourself of body-consciousness and defeat Maya. Recognise your like-minded companions and fly on the wings of pure thought. Become completely detached from our body-conscious world, and give blessings

through soul-conscious thoughts, words and
feelings. Remove the sorrow of all souls everywhere
through the compassion of unconditional love and
truth. By removing the limitations on yourself
you empower others.

Be an angel.

flying free

The Soul's resolve strengthened daily. She knew
that the healing of the Heart and Mind, and the
healing of the world, depended on her union with
divine love. She felt the clarity and power of her
pure surrender to the will of God. The Heart and
Mind were safe and secure once more; cocooned
within the Soul they felt light, loved and contented.
Unshakeable peace and happiness had accompanied
their detachment from the body-consciousness of
the world. They knew that they could only help
the world as they developed disinterest in it. By
emptying themselves of desires and attachments
they were filled with divine love, and radiated
compassion to all souls.

No further words were exchanged between the
Heart, the Mind, the Soul and the Intellect. They
shared a feeling of absolute purity and the power of

divine love. Gone were the feelings of attachment
to the body and the fetters of ego. Even the final
subtle hurdles of ego, the feelings of 'I' and 'mine',
had dissolved. Only a sense of being an instrument
of God's love and truth remained.

They became one with all. They rose blissfully
beyond the feelings of their body, towards a subtle
realm of light. As they were drawn upwards they saw
a shadowy figure standing alone on a battlefield, and
they realised the lone figure was Maya, surrounded
by death and destruction. At her feet lay her five
lieutenants, the five vices. Anger, lust, greed,
attachment and ego were all dead, and Maya stood
powerless without them. A last fading impression
of Maya was of her saluting their victory as they
ascended towards the light of the subtle region.
The Soul had a resounding sense of victory, bliss
and liberation. Drawn towards the power of God
she experienced the pure light of her body and the
deep awareness that she had become an angel.

At that moment she witnessed a multitude
of angels the world over being drawn into the
dimension of light. Each angel was responding
to the call of time, each had attained victory over
Maya and the five vices, and each had recognised
God's task. Each angel was complete and healed,
and was bringing healing to the world. Symbolic of

union, a million angels linked hands and brought the subtle region of purity and light down to the physical plane where Maya desperately held on in her final stronghold. Trapped in the vices, the souls of the world were still in bondage to Maya. Angry and threatened, Maya became a storm, and the earth shook while she adopted her most fearful forms. Desperate souls everywhere looked towards the light, recognising truth through the purity and consciousness of angels who revealed the path to divine love. The shackles of the vices were released from every soul and the experience of liberation swept away their sorrow. Flying free, all souls returned to God. The realm of light contracted to an infinitely small point and the souls returned home. Maya had been defeated, and the world glowed in the golden light of truth and divinity as a new community emerged.

meditation commentary: healing the world

In my mind I see before me the globe of the world. I allow my heart and soul to become unlimited and I tune into the state of my world. My world is crying out

for peace, especially the many souls who are enduring
war or natural calamity. My world is desperate for joy,
especially those who are suffering from disease or
emotional trauma. My world is crying out for love,
especially those who are experiencing loss, conflict or
loneliness. For so many our world is no longer a place
of peace and love. Our quality of life is diminished
under the influence of inappropriate values and selfish
actions.

I look upon my world with mercy and compassion
and I create a pure wish for the world to be healed.
With my strength of spirit I send to the world the light
and energy of peace. With my loving heart I surround
my world with loving feelings and good wishes. With the
conviction of pure values I create a sincere wish for us all
to live and work together in a loving community, living in
the highest spiritual values of respect and co-operation.

With my generous heart and pure spirit I unite with
the divine presence and love of God. Together we bless
our world. I sense God's peace and love passing through
me and caressing the world, nurturing each and every
soul so that they can restore their own purity, peace
and power.

In my mind I see a joyful world — a world full of
peace and love, a world without sorrow, where there
is only the exchange of love and respect.

I believe in the possibility of such a world. I know

our world will once again shine with grace. I recognise that I play a part in bringing this world into being. I keep love and respect shining in my heart always. I keep peace and truth in my spirit forever.

inner

healing

and self-

transformation

a sixty-day course
for healing

$\mathcal{P}$art Two of this book is a two-month meditation
course which develops the themes we have discussed
so far. From my study of Raja Yoga, this course is
designed to engender healing and self-transformation.
As it is also a study think of yourself as a student,
but remember that these teachings are not mine;
their source is universal and they belong to you.
As affirmations they aim to change your perspective
of who you are and what is real. You will discover
a new and exhilarating world of your own creation.
You will learn to detach yourself from negativity,
be easy-going and develop compassion. The course
will help you to develop your spiritual powers, have
strength and flexibility and become a messenger
of peace to the world. Above all you will discover

the source of love and experience its values in this ever-changing world.

In Neale Donald Walsch's trilogy *Conversations with God*, 'God' uses the term 'All That You Really Are' to describe the original nature of spirit.[1] I particularly liked this term and have adapted it for use in the meditations. It equates with the principal teaching of Raja Yoga, which is that you should become soul-conscious (All That You Are) rather than body-conscious (All That You Are Not).

Before studying Raja Yoga I was inspired by a meditation course called *A Course in Miracles*.[2] The course you are about to experience here is presented in a similar style and consists of sixty daily lessons. To gain their full benefit you should set aside time every morning for meditation and also be prepared to practise each lesson throughout the day, even if you are at work. If you lack experience in meditation, don't worry. You do not need to be good at meditating to benefit from the course. If you are not experienced in meditating, I recommend you listen to the meditation commentaries on the

---

[1]   Walsch, Neale Donald, *Conversations with God*, Hodder and Stoughton, London 1998.
[2]   Foundation for Inner Peace, *A Course in Miracles*, Viking Press, New York 1996.

companion CD, *Healing Heart and Soul*. Commentaries are useful while you are learning to meditate. They feed your mind and spirit with positive suggestions, which makes you calmer and more receptive.

Don't worry if you find some of the lessons abstract or occasionally feel resistance in the early stages. It is not necessary to understand all the lessons to benefit from them. They are intended to challenge you to see the world differently. It is not essential to complete the course in two months. You may choose to concentrate on one lesson for a few days or you may want to take a break from the course for a while. However, I believe you will receive the most benefit if you take the course over sixty days. Make a commitment to yourself and be disciplined, but do what is right for you and take the course at your own pace. Most of all enjoy the experience.

1

Nothing is as it appears.

To see the world as it is we must first re-establish our true identity. Through the body we become vulnerable, identify with our roles and develop the false security of ego. This influences how we see our world and what we believe about it.

Whatever you see today, tell yourself it is not as it appears. Do this from morning meditation onwards and include everything.

'My daughter is not as she appears.'

'Those trees are not as they appear.'

'My car is not as it appears.'

'This news is not as it appears.'

'This conflict is not as it appears.'

<hr/>

You may feel some resistance to these early exercises. They are designed to break down preconceptions and broaden our perception.

Remember, you don't have to understand all the exercises to benefit from them. You are establishing a dialogue with the self that will lead to truth.

2

I don't understand anything I hear.

We have developed the habit of reacting to
everything we hear about through body-consciousness
and ego. We are influenced by others, form opinions
and develop negative thoughts and feelings.

Apply this lesson to any news or gossip you hear
today. Everything you hear is designed to separate
you from what is true and real. Everyone is
separated from truth. Everything they report reflects
fear and is distorted through body-consciousness.

From your morning meditation onwards be
determined not to form opinions about things
that don't concern you. Your opinions come from
ego and they continue to deceive you.

3

I am not influenced by what others say about me.

We are all influenced by body-consciousness. What others say about us comes from ego not truth. To find truth we need to remain beyond praise and criticism.

In meditation today let go of any hurt feelings you have about what others have said about you. True forgiveness comes through the understanding that those who hurt you were influenced by body-consciousness. From today be aware that people only see weaknesses because of their own fear and ego. Those who defame you need to heal. Don't be influenced by their sickness.

When you receive praise politely accept it, but don't seek it or believe in it. If you become attached to praise it can deceive you, make you arrogant and separate you from truth. Let go of ego and develop self-respect instead.

After your morning meditation maintain your sense of self-respect, and feel peaceful and confident. Observe what people say but don't be influenced by them. Bring yourself back to this lesson when you hear what people say about others. This lesson can also help you recognise how ego influences our perception and attitudes.

4

Nothing that has hurt me was real.

Hurt feelings and sorrow are generated by ego and not our true selves. In the deepest part of our hearts is a place that always remains free of the suffering we go through.

To heal we need only let go of what is false. We need to forgive ourselves for having the wrong kind of thoughts and learn to trust in the divine order of our lives. We are not victims of the world in which we live. Everything that happens to us has a reason or purpose. Anyone who has hurt us was meant to so that we could recognise what is real and true. Send kind thoughts to them as they are still in the darkness from which you are emerging.

Affirm this lesson in your thoughts throughout the day and let go of pain and sorrow. Keep telling yourself, 'Nothing that has hurt me was real.

Forgiveness is my recognition of this.' Reflect on this whenever you have free time. It is not essential that you fully understand this yet as your understanding will deepen throughout the course.

As I see myself, so I see the world.

The world we see is our own creation. For mortal beings the body and ego is truth and their world is a projection of this truth. They see death, segregation and separation. They live in fear, pursuing temporary happiness and self-gratification. The world they project creates an illusion — nothing is real.

In your morning meditation see yourself as an eternal being. Project your awareness to the world by seeing others as eternal beings and create feelings of unity and truth. Remember this lesson at every opportunity throughout your day. See yourself as a child of the divine and others as your brothers and sisters. Sisterhood and brotherhood heal separation.

As I change, the world changes.

When we change our world changes in two ways.
By becoming conscious of the soul we see the world
in a different light. We also become a messenger
of truth for others, inspiring them to change. At
a higher level of consciousness we are co-operating
with God, and all other souls who are becoming
enlightened at this time.

⁓ ⁓

In meditation and throughout your day regularly
think of yourself as a soul. Think of what is needed
in the world now — love, compassion, tolerance,
truth. Adopt these virtues and develop your nature
as an enlightened being. Allow your changing
personality to serve the world.

I choose to experience myself as All That I Am.

Through body and ego we experience ourselves as All That We Are Not. This is why fear governs our lives as we try to affirm our self-esteem, concerned about how others see us. But many of us give up and stop caring about ourselves and how others see us. When we choose to see ourselves as souls, love governs our lives and the intellect acquires the power to discern truth from illusion.

❧

During this lesson and after your morning meditation, remember and repeat the affirmation, 'I choose to experience myself as All That I Am.' Instead of thinking that you have a soul, think that you are a soul and that your body is its vehicle or instrument. Remember that others are souls too, and marvel that you have recognised what they are blind to, for everyone else is still under the illusion of body-consciousness.

Recognising yourself as a soul makes you both great and humble. This is the foundation of true self-respect.

8

I choose to experience a world that reflects All That I Am.

We are used to a world that mirrors the mistaken belief that we are merely a body. By choosing to see ourselves as souls we see beyond the limitations of others with the knowledge that one day they too will awaken. Choose to see a world in divine order where nothing is right or wrong — it simply *is* — and accept that spiritual blindness is the nature of this age.

When you see yourself as a soul you create a world that reflects your spirituality. Your attitude offers the potential for others to change, and you begin to develop a firm, confident sense of self.

— ~ —

From morning meditation adopt the thoughts and feelings of the soul, and choose to see only love, truth, peace and happiness. When you hear of conflict, tragedy, hardship and deception think, 'This is not real and reflects All That I Am Not. It mirrors a false belief. Only that which reflects All That I Am is real.'

9

God loves me as I am.

If we could see ourselves as God sees us we would be truly happy. As divine living energy God sees only truth and has only love for the soul. He never looks at our weaknesses and always sees our beauty and perfection. We are all children of God — no one is denied God's love. We separate ourselves from God by believing that we are principally our body, and by the thoughts that come from ego.

God's vibrations of love, truth, peace and holiness are ever-present; just as we can tune into our favourite radio station, we can tune into God's frequency with our minds. Body-consciousness and ego are on the wrong wavelength and they separate us from the relationship of divine love. When you experience yourself as a soul, you become All That You Are and tune into God's love.

In morning meditation think of yourself as a soul, and accept the love God has for you. Today frequently affirm that 'God loves me as I am, and never sees me as I am not.'

I choose to see myself as God sees me.

*I*n accepting that God sees us As We Are we renew our relationship with the original purity and innocence of the soul. We need not think of our defects and weaknesses. The inner beauty of our virtues and strengths emerge through meditation and contemplation. It is then easy to forgive our mistakes and heal and transform our weaknesses and negativity, using the self-respect that God gives us.

～ ～

From morning meditation and throughout the day, affirm this lesson. Remember to apply it when others treat you in a negative or destructive way, criticising you or undermining your authority. Instead of seeing yourself through their eyes, say to yourself, 'I choose to see myself as God sees me.' In this way you remember your identity as a soul and forgive others their mistakes.

*I choose to see others as God
sees me.*

When we accept God's pure vision of the soul,
we experience love, peace and happiness in our
relationships and connections. This is the basis
for deep self-respect, which gives us the ability
to see beyond our own weaknesses and accept
and understand the weaknesses of others. It is
as though we look through the eyes of God and,
seeing only truth, we extend God's merciful vision
to others.

In morning meditation and every hour of the day
accept God's love for yourself and extend it to
others with this affirmation: 'God sees others as
He sees me. I choose to see in others only what
God sees in me.'

My original religion is peace.

We are created in God's image; our original nature was pure and peaceful. Only body-consciousness, the ego and our actions have changed this.

Enhance the understanding and experience of your spiritual convictions through the realisation that your original nature is that of a peaceful soul. Any other thoughts are deceptions of the body and ego. Today you shall choose truth over illusion.

From today onwards take at least half an hour for morning meditation and practise today's lesson every hour throughout your day. Affirm regularly: 'I am a soul and my original religion is peace.'

My nature emanates from a subtle, eternal point.

To begin meditation we create thoughts to still the mind, bringing us feelings of peace. In deep meditation we experience a sense of oneness and unity, which heals the illusion that we are separated from God, but we retain a sense of who we are and who God is. Within this divine union we retain the feeling of our own identity.

We experience God's nature as an unlimited radiance of love, peace, purity and wisdom through which we come to know our own form. God's nature is always accessible, radiating from a source of immense purity and power. From an infinitely tiny point of light like a star in the night sky, God emanates love and truth. Like the source, our soul is subtle, simple and eternally invisible; a point that radiates our nature and personality.

In today's meditation we remember our form of subtle concentrated energy. Begin by thinking of a point in the middle of a page, then imagine a point in the middle of that point and so on. Now imagine you have reached a point the size of an atom and put a point in the middle of that, and keep going until your soul — the point — is infinitely small and almost non-existent. Welcome to who you are! You have reached your seat of consciousness, where your experiences, thoughts and actions come from, via the instrument of your mind. It is just behind the middle of your forehead.

Visualise yourself as a point of light radiating energy in morning meditation and repeat today's lesson to yourself every hour.

14

My thoughts reflect my awareness.

When we first enter the body we are innocent of the desires, needs and dependencies developed through the body. The soul is completely trusting and incapable of impure or selfish thoughts. It can be happy for no reason. However, we are inexperienced in worldly life which leaves us vulnerable. In a few short years the soul surrenders its identity to the body, and life experience conditions it to be selective with love, trust and acceptance. Happiness becomes dependent on fulfilling our desires or having our needs met, and this is reflected in our thoughts.

The next few exercises are designed to make you more aware of the quality of your thoughts and to help you understand the impact your thoughts have on your life. You will also develop the power of your intellect to discern wasteful or negative thoughts from positive thoughts, and this improves your capacity to decide how you experience life.

From your morning meditation and throughout the day make firm this lesson by repeating to yourself every hour, 'My thoughts reflect my awareness.' Reflect on the types of thoughts you have and what results from them. Did your thoughts make you feel worried or concerned? Have you been angry or upset? What thought created this experience?

15

Healing resides in the thoughts I choose.

We have only suffered through the consciousness by which we perceive situations. With this understanding we can create thoughts to heal our lives. No one has ever died and no one has hurt us. Our pain and suffering arises from perceiving as true what is not real. When we choose to think about what is eternal we see the truth. Our healing resides in these thoughts.

In today's meditation develop the idea that you create your experiences through your thoughts. Be aware of the power of your mind. Decide not to allow external influences to dictate your thoughts and feelings. Don't be influenced by the opinions, attitudes and negativity of others. Become the master of your own thoughts, experiences and destiny.

From morning meditation onwards affirm the thought every hour, 'Healing resides in the thoughts I choose and only what has healed is real.'

16

Hurtful thoughts are illusions of ego.

*W*e create ego after coming under the spell of the body. Ego's foundation is fear. Everything we perceive through ego is false and separates us from All That We Are. Through ego we suffer. When we express hurtful thoughts to others through our words and actions we position our ego against another's. Neither is real, and both parties are hurt by the interaction.

Choose to let go of past hurts, understanding that they are the result of mistaken identity. Concentrate on knowing yourself as All That You Are — a peaceful soul — and renew your true identity. Recognise that those who have hurt you were under the influence of what is not real, and forgive them. Forgive yourself too.

— ◆ —

From morning meditation and throughout the day, remind yourself: 'Hurtful thoughts are illusions that come from ego.' Decide that you will not think or say anything hurtful to or about others. Know yourself as a benevolent spirit.

17

Positive thoughts are true expressions of spirit.

By filling our minds with thoughts of our eternal nature and form we experience peace, happiness and motivation. Nourishing ourselves daily with these thoughts breaks the negative expressions of ego and the habits of body-consciousness gradually. This is the aim of Raja Yoga meditation: to reaffirm spirit, to eliminate vices and the dependencies of ego, while imbibing the original virtues of the soul.

Keep your thoughts positive by affirming that you are a soul and this is your body. The body is simply a vehicle driven by the soul. It is also an instrument through which you can bring relief or happiness to others. See others as souls who have forgotten who they are. Your example will shine and enlighten many lost and weary travellers.

Every time you affirm this lesson today be aware that positive thoughts are peaceful thoughts. At least three times today, spend one minute in silence and still your mind. Repeat to yourself, 'I am a peaceful soul. Only my positive thoughts are real.'

Negative thoughts arise from fear.

Only peace and purity are real. When we are healed we know only the thoughts and feelings of our original nature. These emanate from love and are reflected in our words and actions. Before we separated from our original nature, negative thoughts were non-existent.

Negative thoughts bring worries and pain to ourselves and others. Fear is an illusion built on beliefs that associate our identity with our bodies. When you affirm your true identity — that you are a peaceful soul — you let go of fear and realise all negativity is an illusion.

In morning meditation and every hour today, affirm: 'Negative thoughts arise from fear. They are not real.'

As for yesterday's exercise, spend one minute in silence three times today to affirm: 'I am a peaceful soul. Only my positive thoughts are real.'

*Waste thoughts are a waste of time
and energy.*

Waste thoughts are habits of body-consciousness.
They don't cause pain the way negative thoughts
do, but they waste time and energy. We have
cultivated the habit of thinking of others or of
situations that don't involve us, and of imagining
situations that don't exist. These thoughts drain
our energy. Most people complain of fatigue by
the time they reach their mid-thirties — their
minds are all over the place. Develop the power
to concentrate your mind by eliminating waste
thoughts and sustaining your energy.

— ∿ —

Observe your mind from today onwards and detect
waste thoughts. As soon as you form these thoughts
or develop unimportant opinions, put a full stop on
your mind. Withdraw your mind into the awareness
of your eternal form. Now you are using the power

of the mind to withdraw from external influences that have dictated your thoughts and feelings.

When your mind wanders in meditation it is mainly distracted by waste thoughts. Affirm to yourself, 'Waste thoughts are a waste of time and energy. Only positive thoughts of my eternal nature are real.' At three different times today have a minute of silent reflection, 'I am a peaceful soul,' and withdraw into peaceful feelings.

I have the power to discern truth from illusion.

We develop the power of our intellect to discern truth from illusion by seeing ourselves as All That We Are — peaceful souls — and looking at the world with this knowledge. The power to discern truth from illusion allows us to withdraw our thoughts from waste or negativity and use our minds in constructive and creative ways.

——— ~ ———

As you look at the scenes before you today remember All That You Are. Withdraw into your true self and become a detached observer of each scene of your day. Keep your thoughts focused on positive feelings of truth and identity. Affirm the day's lesson every hour and in three one-minute periods of silent reflection.

I forgive and set myself free.

*I*n truth, there is nothing for us to forgive. We simply need to understand and let go of the past. Words or actions performed under the influence of body-consciousness are mistakes. Think of them as not real. When we understand this we easily forgive past wrongs, and see everyone, even ourselves, as innocent and blameless. This is merciful vision.

The wounded heart is reluctant to let go. If you can't forgive others they continue to affect you. You are tied to them and they control your feelings. When you forgive them they remain accountable for their actions but you are freed from their influence on your life. When you forgive yourself you free yourself of the guilt that ties you to the past — a past in which nothing 'real' happened.

After morning meditation, and hourly throughout the day, practise this lesson for those you wish to forgive, including yourself. Understand that forgiveness is for you. It allows you to let go of the past, freeing you in the present. During three short meditation periods sit in silence and remember, 'Through forgiveness I am a peaceful soul.'

22

I let go and allow love.

When we let go of the past we let go of fear that has governed our lives. The absence of fear creates space in our lives which is filled by unconditional love. When we forgive and let go we experience divine love, which heals our soul. This healing is ever-present, waiting for us; we just have to choose it.

Allow love into your life today. Love yourself and have compassion for all beings. Feel a closeness to God in your love. Don't try to control it — simply experience feelings of love, peace and unity.

Focus on letting go, surrender and love in your morning meditation. Hourly throughout the day affirm the lesson, 'I let go and allow love. I am one with all and one with God.' In the three short periods of silence during your day sense God's love reaching your heart, filling you with truth.

23

I accept everything as it is and become still.

*A*cceptance and unconditional love are strong features of the healed heart and soul. We are accustomed to judging who is right and who is wrong, which is filtered through our ego. In this course of meditations we are breaking this habit to develop a new perspective. Nothing is right or wrong in the drama — *it just is*. When we accept this we develop the clarity of truth and the power of spiritual judgement which allows us to act according to our highest nature.

In today's lesson, practise acceptance every hour after your morning meditation. Become a detached observer. Tell yourself that nothing is right or wrong. Don't form opinions about things that aren't your responsibility, and don't listen to opinions about others. Accept everything and everyone and become still. If you feel some resistance remember that the aim of this course is to identify with spirit and to persuade your own mind to see through spirit. During your three periods of silence today remember yourself as a peaceful soul, become very still and accept yourself.

Acceptance is my purpose now.

With acceptance we have no tension or fear, and are not influenced by the past. Acceptance requires forgiveness and trust in the unfolding drama of life. Everything is in divine order and reflects our destiny. With acceptance we allow love for all souls into our lives, and become the embodiment of love itself.

Practise trust and forgiveness as well as acceptance in today's lesson. 'Acceptance, trust and forgiveness are my purpose now. All is in divine order and I am free from limited ways of thinking.'

From morning meditation and hourly throughout the day, affirm today's lesson of acceptance. Spend three short periods in silence with the thought, 'I accept the divine order of destiny and the plan of the drama.'

Acceptance gives me the power to tolerate.

When our tolerance is the product of ego we experience internal tension while we put up with a situation or someone's attitude or behaviour. We think we are tolerant, but really we are holding onto and suppressing a grievance. Through the illusion of ego we react to what is not real about the person who makes us feel intolerant. Acceptance separates us from All That They Are Not and we see them as souls acting under the influence of fear and ego.

Real tolerance comes from love. It contains spiritual knowledge, acceptance and understanding. It is without tension. When you use real tolerance others experience it as peace and power, and you are more likely to get their co-operation.

— ⁓ —

After morning meditation and every hour throughout the day, affirm the lesson: 'Acceptance gives me the power to tolerate through love and understanding. I only see what's true and real.'

In three short periods of silence reflect on yourself as a peaceful soul who brings peace to the world.

Truth is my holiness revealed.

We become holy when we know and accept
All That We Are and reflect this in our vision
on the world. Truth gives the soul the power to
accommodate any personality or situation while
revealing peace and purity to the world. Truth
gives us the courage to open our hearts to love
without expectations or conditions. When the
soul is filled with truth and the heart is open,
the spirit shines through and reveals its
holiness.

   Accept you are holy and be true to your higher
purpose. Think only of truth today and have the
courage to open your heart. Many people fear this
because they have been hurt in the past. They
become misers with their hearts. First stabilise
yourself with truth and your heart will not be so
vulnerable. Your fears are not real; they are
whispers of ego.

Today begin meditating on holiness for half an hour. Open your heart to the holiness of God's truth and love for you. Then give God's truth and love to the world. Give the world what you receive from God. Affirm every hour: 'Truth is my holiness revealed. I let go of fear and holiness shines through my open heart.'

In three two-minute periods of silence through the day repeat the thoughts of your morning meditation.

Through my holiness I bless the world with love.

When we truly understanding our eternal spiritual identity without holding any grievances our nature becomes a blessing. We all have the potential to bless the world with our thoughts, kindness and words. Holiness is unconditional love, revealing spiritual truth and power. Our holiness reveals love as a blessing on the world.

Today take at least half an hour for morning meditation and create the experience of healing the world with divine feelings of love and peace. Be at one with the divine and extend feelings of holiness to awaken the sleeping souls of the world. Practice this thought every hour and during three two-minute periods of silence.

God is the source of my holiness.

Holiness was our original nature. Our soul was innocent, pure and untouched by fear or mistrust. Only our original nature is true — nothing else is real — and only God retains the blueprint of our original nature of peace and purity. When we return to God we receive the holiness that makes us like Him.

In the next few exercises, through daily practices of remembering the divine, you are encouraged to connect to the source of holiness. Anything created by ego is not holy, and so it is not real. Only our holiness is real.

Try to extend your morning meditation to forty minutes from this day on. Find peace in your eternal form and open yourself to experience the divine. Tell yourself you are one with God and ask

God to reveal His holiness to your soul. In your hourly reflection today, and in three two-minute periods of silence, remember, 'God is the source of my holiness. I am one with the divine and accept only that which is real.'

29

God's love dissolves ego.

We can choose truth or illusion. Truth heals our
heart and soul. Ego hurts us. Ego was created for
self-gratification and to counter our fear and
insecurity. All suffering and pain is false reality,
based on ego's determination that *it* is real.
Through ego we hold on to the life we know and
deny God. Ego's hold over our feelings of identity
results in suffering, but no aspect of suffering is
real or permanent. When you understand this you
will be healed.

In your forty minutes of meditation today visualise
yourself receiving the light of God's love and merge
with it as though you are merging deep into an
ocean of love and light. Imagine yourself dissolving
into the light of God's love until you are one with
love. Whisper to God, 'I die to Your love.' (This

'I' is the ego dying in divine love.) Repeat this affirmation hourly throughout the day and spend three two-minute periods of silence absorbed in this affirmation.

I am as God created me.

Whatever God created in us is real, whereas we created ego and separated from God. Nothing about ego is true. To see ourselves as God's creation we must separate ourselves from delusion — the perception of ego — and allow God to reach our soul.

— ∾ ∾ —

Be simple today. In forty minutes of morning meditation imagine God's divine presence around you, and have a sense of 'allowing God'. Don't resist; simply accept who you are in God's loving heart. Let go and surrender to the thought, 'I am as God created me.' Throughout the day, on the hour and during three periods of silence, recreate this thought and feelings of letting go and surrender.

My salvation lies in God.

Salvation is to live in the peace and happiness
of spirit. God's plan for salvation is to reveal who
we are and to re-establish the original self. When
we accept God we accept the drama of life as
divine. This acceptance makes way for peace and
stability in our lives and we are able to observe
every scene with detachment. Elevated thoughts
of our eternal identity sustain our happiness and
keep us connected to God's loving nature.

Salvation lies in the death of ego. This recognition
and its acceptance brings the expression of truth
into our lives.

In morning meditation today imagine or visualise
a grey cloud around you, separating you from the
warm rays of God's wisdom. Gradually you see this
cloud lift and rays of light penetrate your soul. The

cloud can represent any aspect of ego, pain or suffering from which you wish to free yourself. Repeat the affirmation, 'my salvation lies in God', during meditation, hourly throughout the day and during each of your three two-minute periods of silence. If you wish, add 'God's wisdom frees me.'

32

*I see a new world based on
my salvation.*

When we free ourselves from illusion we begin to
see the possibility of a world based on such freedom.
Its values reflect simplicity, peace, purity and
happiness. A world based on our salvation is free
from conflict and grievances. As we learn the
authentic vision of truth and how to see beyond
what isn't real, we begin to transform the world
in which we live.

Your salvation is the recognition and experience
of truth. It comes from living in God's heart and
from the power of this relationship. Your salvation
comes from co-operating with God's purpose to
reveal Himself. This co-operation is the foundation
of a new world based on your salvation.

———

In your morning meditation imagine yourself freed
from everything that limits your consciousness. Let

go of your body and relationships and say, 'I can only see You now.' Visualise God as the seed, a tiny point of light emanating power. Imagine yourself as a mirror-image of God, a tiny soul receiving His light and power. You are completely special. God's loving vision is falling on you and His purpose is to create a world based on your salvation. In your hourly reflection and periods of silence today absorb this thought.

33

Co-operating with God is my only purpose.

Truth and illusion cannot exist together. When we are enlightened and develop the insight to recognise and discern truth we can choose it and act according to it. Many people have enlightening experiences but stay with the ways of the world. Lacking courage, they choose what is familiar — illusion. Those who have the courage to step away from this world also step away from its vices and become children of God.

When you co-operate with God your surrender makes you a sample of truth, and an instrument of peace in this world. You help to create the consciousness required for a divine community to emerge from a civilisation that depends on Maya (illusion). Nothing remains for you in this world. Once you have the courage to accept this you will recognise that truth means co-operating with God. God depends on you. How else can His truth be known?

During your forty minutes of meditation today allow yourself to become a child of God and receive unlimited love from your divine parent. Imagine the nurturing love of a mother sustaining your soul and the loving directions of a father teaching you to become like Him. Say to your divine parent, 'I surrender to Your love and become like You.' In your hourly reflections today affirm, 'Co-operating with God is my only purpose now.' Spend three two-minute periods of silence feeling that God, your constant companion, is empowering you.

34

All is divine in the drama.

When we have a spiritual perspective we know that everything has a reason, a purpose or a meaning, and we stop asking questions such as, 'Why did this happen?' and 'What is the reason for this?' We become observers of the drama.

Serenity emerges from our acceptance and instead of being the embodiment of questions we become the embodiment of understanding. This is not blind faith but a way of learning from the world at the same time as becoming liberated from it.

The next few lessons encourage you to look at life as a drama enacted on the world stage. All souls have their roles, whether heroes or villains, supporting cast or main actors, and each soul plays their part perfectly. These exercises allow you to detach yourself from the scenes as an observer, and to develop the power to tolerate and accommodate everything in your life.

In your forty minutes of morning meditation today
see yourself as a soul. Visualise your soul as a tiny
point of light in the centre of your forehead. Turn
your attention to the souls of the world, visualising
scenes from around the world. View these scenes
with detachment. Without reaction or judgement
simply affirm to yourself, 'All is divine in the drama.
I have nothing to fear.' Throughout the day let go
of your need to judge others with this statement,
and recall this state of acceptance in your three
two-minute periods of silence.

35

'Drama, sweet drama.'

When we understand and apply the lesson of the 'drama' we are less affected by circumstance, chaos and injustice. When we apply this lesson to our own life we can retreat to the essence of the soul rather than feeling challenged or disturbed by the world. The more upheaval there is around us the more peaceful we can become. The power lies in understanding that this drama is just a game in which 'nothing matters much and most things don't matter at all'.

According to chaos theory, maximum order emerges from maximum disorder. The more chaotic the world becomes the more hope there is for divine order. Rather than losing hope develop the conviction that the world changes as you change. The future of the drama is the defeat of Maya (ego's illusion) and the re-emergence of truth.

In today's meditation spend forty minutes seeing yourself as a being of light, seated in the centre of your forehead, detached from your body. Let the problems of the world pass through your mind without attaching any emotion or importance to them and say to yourself, 'Drama, sweet drama.' Now do the same with your immediate problems and concerns. Practise this hourly throughout the day and during your three two-minute periods of silence. Whenever a challenge presents itself from now on remember these three words, 'Drama, sweet drama.' Withdraw, be peaceful and observe with detachment.

36

Nothing matters.

$\mathcal{E}$go attaches importance to things and separates us from love and simplicity. It is difficult for ego to accept there is nothing wrong with the world because this is a denial of its own creation. Ego resists ideas that challenge its existence. Everything that seems wrong or that seems to matter is a projection of ego and is not real. The lesson of 'nothing matters' separates us from ego (what's not real), allowing love and simplicity to re-emerge.

Apply this lesson throughout the rest of the course. Add to it the three words, 'drama, sweet drama.' When challenges arise think, 'Nothing matters … Drama, sweet drama.' Become conscious of yourself as a soul and of the dimension of spiritual light each time you do this. Everything becomes simple when you eliminate ego's complexity.

In today's exercise repeat the previous lesson with the added words 'nothing matters'. Don't trivialise situations that matter to everyone else, but experience life in a new way through the realisation of your soul.

37

The present scenes are not real.

*F*rom the moment we lose our spiritual innocence reality is based on body-consciousness. Ego, the projection of body-consciousness, casts a shroud over the soul, conditioning the soul to see what is false as true. The soul forgets who it is and forgets God, believing that a world seen through fear is the real world.

The present scenes of the drama have been created through the body-consciousness and ego of six billion souls. At no other point in the drama has there been so many forms of delusion and deception. Once aware of drama you have the power to pack up your past thoughts and recreate yourself through spiritual knowledge. One of the first steps is to recognise your soul and turn its loving vision on the world. This is a great challenge to Maya or illusion, ego's creation.

Repeat the meditation and exercises of the last two days again. Add the extra dimension of today's lesson, 'the present scenes are not real' to 'drama, sweet drama' and 'nothing matters'.

38

I have no interest in a world separated from truth.

The ultimate victory of the soul is complete disinterest in ego's creation. Fear is behind ego's creation. When we develop disinterest in what the world has become, we let go of our fear and reawaken unconditional love. Ego draws us into a complex web of external dependencies and fills the heart with attachments and desires. Ultimately, there is no room in the heart for truth. When we develop disinterest in worldly things we create space in our hearts for spiritual love.

The scenes before you are not real. You are developing detachment and a creative disinterest in those scenes. As you do this you become an image that reflects truth. To help this world rediscover true love and understanding you must first detach yourself from what it has become.

In today's forty-minute meditation contemplate ego's forms. Think of the many role identities we have; the clashes and conflicts; the influences of gender, politics and religion; the effect of vices such as attachment, greed and anger. Think how souls get trapped in the expansion of these matters, and come to think of this as reality. Remember you are a peaceful soul, full of love, mercy and compassion. Know this is reality. Apply the lesson of the day, 'I have no interest in a world separated from truth,' and create an image to help you envisage ego dissolving in the light of truth. Every hour throughout your day and in three periods of silence, repeat the lesson and its imagery, and apply it to the circumstances of your day.

39

The future is merged in the present.

The drama is destined to evolve in its own way. While you accept this you must also know that you have a role in the drama. Our actions and reactions create each new scene that appears in the drama. We live in the present and our future emerges from it.

The drama is predestined, so become a detached observer of its scenes. You are now playing a spiritual role and are not influenced by the passing scenes. Your intellect is developing the power to discern truth from illusion and your actions are connected to revealing truth from the drama. Truth, divinity and a community based on these principles are emerging in the drama. These result from the actions of enlightened beings. In a seeming paradox the unfolding drama is fixed and predestined, but it depends on souls recognising what is real and expressing this in their free will.

In today's meditation, hourly throughout the day and in your three periods of silence, imagine a community living in perfect harmony, with perfect peace and happiness. Everyone is co-operative and there is no vocabulary for stress or conflict. Believe that this community is emerging out of the present human chaos. Understand that by co-operating with truth you create this scene. Remember: 'The future is merged in the present.'

40

*The drama reveals the fortune of
all souls.*

There are no victims or perpetrators in a play,
only actors playing their parts. You can't see the
full story of any soul in the script. No one has ever
died in the drama and all souls have always existed.
Whatever happens to someone is a reflection of
their past actions or is creating their future. All
souls are accountable for their actions (karma)
through the body. Reincarnation and the philosophy
of rebirth explains the interrelationship of karma
with the drama you see. Obstacles and difficulties
compel a soul to develop new strengths.

Today look at souls in a new light. If they are
experiencing misfortune such as disease, trauma or
persecution, understand that they are not victims
and they are not being punished. The drama is
revealing a past they are now being liberated from.
They may think of this as suffering, but it is healing
through the destruction of ego. All suffering is

temporary. Within it lies salvation and a way to truth. The drama also reveals the good fortune of souls. You might not think that they deserve their fortune yet it is accumulated in their past karma.

— —

In meditation today, in your hourly reflection and in your periods of silence focus on this insight: 'I know not what I see and judge not what I hear. I am simply an observer listening to the deep secrets of the drama, which reveals the fortune of souls. Nothing influences me for I know myself as All That I Am eternally.'

41

I create my own fortune.

*H*ow we experience the future of the drama is connected to what we are doing now. When our actions are elevated they reflect spiritual truth, peace and happiness, and they plant the seed of a community living by these principles. These actions are a credit in our karmic account and we reap their rewards. Elevated thoughts connect our hearts and minds to God. In healing ourselves through God we look only to what is real and become instruments of healing in the world.

Our fortune is twofold. Firstly, chaotic or destructive scenes no longer disturb us because we understand them. We recognise that destructive scenes are essential to a world healing through crisis. Secondly, we become part of creating a new world order and have a direct relationship with God.

— —

In meditation today and during your three periods
of silence, contemplate a world healing through
your recognition of truth. Visualise divine love
surrounding you with light and imagine this love
filling you and flowing to the whole world. Say to
yourself, 'Souls of the world are blind and trapped.
I now create my fortune by freeing them from
suffering and illusion.' Be aware of your fortune
by being merciful throughout the day. Show respect
and accept everyone. Repeat this lesson hourly.
Understand that you are a rare soul to have such
recognition of spirit and purpose.

42

Forgiveness frees me in the drama.

Detached from the passing scenes of the drama we are able to observe everything in an impartial way. Everything is part of a divine plan. It was only our ignorance that led to us giving or taking sorrow from the circumstances of our lives. Knowledge of the drama and forgiveness heal the heart and mind and make us free.

In today's lesson consider occasions on which you felt hurt or neglected and on which you hurt others. Contemplate and develop the awareness: 'Everything was due to ignorance and misunderstanding. All is now forgiven and I hold no grievances.' The deepest aspect of forgiveness is that there is nothing to forgive and your continuing grievances keep you shackled to the past. Let go of grievances, and through acts of forgiveness free yourself from the past.

— ~ —

In forty minutes of meditation today devote some time to visualising forgiveness. Forgive those who hurt you; they remain accountable for their actions anyway. The law of karma means that they will have to settle their accounts in their own time and in their own way. Forgiving them simply frees you from holding a grievance that hurts you. Forgive yourself too; free yourself from guilt and recognise that this is all you need to move on. Hourly throughout the day remember: 'Forgiveness frees me in the drama.' During your three periods of silence reflect on letting go of your grievances.

43

Forgiveness is divine loving vision.

With freedom and forgiveness we let go of grievances and release ourselves from fear. We can look on the drama not only impartially but with confidence and loving vision. We become the embodiment of acceptance, knowing we are witnessing the effects of ego and past actions (karma). Karmic accounts are being settled. The world awaits enlightenment. Through acceptance and divine loving vision we offer truth to the world.

Turn your forgiveness on the world today in the form of acceptance and divine love. This is your gift to troubled souls who live the illusion as truth. Think deeply about this: 'Fear is all I have to forgive; fear is the source of illusion.'

Instead of giving limited forgiveness to the self and others, today's lesson is about giving this quality to the whole world. When we use forgiveness to liberate ourselves from Maya (ego, illusion) our acceptance spreads to the world. Loving acceptance contains the power of realisation and transformation.

During your forty-minute meditation today accept the world as it is and envisage pure love passing through you to those lost in the illusion. Recreate this feeling every hour with the thought, 'Forgiveness is divine loving vision.' In three periods of two-minute silences remember that 'Fear is all I have to forgive. Fear is the source of illusion.'

44

Understanding and forgiveness give me power.

Through acceptance and the divine loving vision of forgiveness, we have the power to tolerate anything. Tolerance is a sign of power emerging from the soul. Distinct from worldly tolerance, which implies suppressed tension, this natural tolerance is a state of love and acceptance and understanding the drama. The power to tolerate allows us to remain simple, unaffected and constantly loving.

—◆ ◆—

In today's lesson affirm hourly, 'Understanding and forgiveness give me power.' Add to this, 'Tolerance keeps me simple, unaffected and loving.'

In your morning meditation spend forty minutes visualising the light of God touching your spirit with truth and divinity. Accept yourself as true and divine in God's loving eyes. Turn your self-acceptance on the world and extend this feeling of acceptance and love to everyone, everywhere. In three two-minute periods of silence today extend your love and acceptance of yourself to everyone.

45

My power comes from self-respect.

Natural tolerance is an expression of love and
self-respect. When we see ourselves as souls we
experience the part of ourselves that is worthy of
God's love, the real part of ourselves. Feelings of
unworthiness and arrogance about achievements
are the whispers of ego. To end these we need to
accept ourselves as worthy of God's love; this is
self-respect, the right way of loving the self. It is
how we receive God's forgiveness and become
His child.

When you have self-respect nothing can harm
you. You are comfortable with whatever others
think or say about you, and you have no desire to
think or speak of others' weaknesses. With God's
love you don't seek praise or recognition because
you are content. Experiencing yourself as worthy in
the eyes of God you are liberated from emotional
needs. You are constantly content and serene.

In meditation today surrender yourself to God by accepting His love as a child. See God accepting you on the throne of His heart and hear God's words in the silence of your mind: 'My child, you have a right to My love eternally. I am with you always.'

Each hour, and in your three two-minute periods of silence repeat the lesson, 'My power comes from self-respect.' Then add, 'And self-respect comes from recognising my right to God's love.'

46

Whatever happens is good.

The lesson of the drama must be firmly in our hearts if we are to maintain peace, love, respect, tolerance and forgiveness. <u>Whatever happens is good.</u> When we can apply this to the worst-case scenario we defeat Maya, but Maya will continue to challenge us. Maya's strategy is to make us reactive through body-consciousness and ego, and to make us believe that death, deprivation and victimisation are real. Apply the words, 'drama, sweet drama,' to situations followed by the lesson for today: 'Whatever happens is good.'

———— ————

In today's meditation see yourself as a soul and your body as an instrument moving through the scenes of your life. Firmly feel that, 'whatever happens is good,' and, 'I am only upset when I apply truth to All That is Not Real.' When 'bad' things happen simply accept that accounts of past actions (karmic accounts), yours included, are being settled and that the drama is beneficial to all souls. When the burden of karma is diminished we find our true purpose and recognise God. Affirm the day's lesson every hour and in your three two-minute periods of silence.

47

As a soul I co-operate with God alone.

Understanding the drama is the key to our salvation. It frees our soul and allows us to be peaceful under circumstances that previously disturbed us. When we know truth from illusion we recognise God's role and co-operate in the establishment of a world of truth. We are drawn closer to God's principal desires — our happiness, our liberation from Maya and world transformation.

Use your conscience and the discerning power of intellect to recognise truth and act solely according to its directions. Never cause anyone sorrow. Respect yourself and give respect to others. See everyone as souls — children of God — and have the loving vision of sisterhood and brotherhood. Make your every thought, word and action elevated, reflecting your eternal identity of a soul and your original nature of peace. By co-operating with God your real self becomes visible, ego's influence dies and God is revealed through you.

——— ——

In meditation today visualise God as a loving light. Be drawn into God's light until you are merged in God's love. Then say these words: 'Your love and truth are one. Recognising truth I co-operate with you alone.' In silence, following these words, feel God's vision and power filling your soul with pure, divine, unconditional love. Hold this conversation within you throughout the day. Hourly and in your three two-minute periods of silence make this your silent prayer for holiness.

48

Co-operating with God gives me power.

When you become conscious of yourself as a soul, you attend to the original virtues of your character. You decorate yourself with love, peace, tolerance, compassion, gentleness, humility and self-respect. As you do so your recognition of God becomes clearer and your power of co-operation grows. You finish with ego and its dependence on the five vices — lust, arrogance, attachment, greed and anger — to protect or satisfy yourself. When you choose virtues and reject vices you are co-operating with God.

By co-operating with God you offer the world what He has given you. To donate what you have received — truth, happiness, the power of peace — ensure your motives are pure and co-operate with others. Receiving co-operation from others is the sign that your power of co-operation has increased. Your power of co-operation makes others contented and empowers them to transform their lives through spirituality.

— ❦ —

In forty minutes of meditation today relax your body and detach from the physical world. Go to the source of God in your visualisation. Imagine an infinitely small point radiating pure love. Envisage this love as light reaching all the souls of the world, removing sorrow, revealing truth and creating happiness. Draw God's love into yourself and co-operate with God by allowing His love to reach the world through you. Envisage many souls like yourself doing the same and feel a sense of unity of purpose. Within this union experience the power of being God's helper. Repeat this visualisation during your three two-minutes of silence today and affirm the day's lesson every hour.

49

Co-operating with God is holiness.

We cannot co-operate with God through ego or body-consciousness. By accepting God we surrender and let go of ego, returning to All That We Are — pure, eternally divine beings with the powers of love and self-transformation. Accepting God is the first step. To co-operate with God absorb His qualities into the self and extend these to others. We become holy when we stop separating ourselves from God's nature and His task in our thoughts and feelings.

— ◆ ◆ —

In meditation today have a conversation with God. Make the topic 'surrender' and say, 'I let go of everything that is not real, my name and form, the roles I play, and all relationships other than ours. I let go of ego, my creation, and with it my worries, concerns and feelings of responsibility.'

Imagine these are a handful of rice you sacrifice into a fire. Then repeat over and over, 'I surrender to You. I am Your child. We are one.' Be silent and allow yourself to experience the loving form of God touching your heart and healing the world.

Hourly throughout the day affirm to yourself, 'Co-operating with God is holiness.' In three two-minute periods of silence repeat your surrender from the morning meditation.

50

I surrender through complete acceptance.

Complete acceptance of All That I Am is the soul's salvation. Surrender is the death of ego, limitation and illusion. When we have surrendered nothing draws us to false truths. We become clear, accurate, simple, powerful extensions of divine will. With complete acceptance of yourself and God, your pure thoughts carry the power of love, truth and transformation.

Acceptance is a pure state of being which radiates from your soul. All sense of separation is healed and God radiates through your union. In this way acceptance makes you a humble instrument with the knowledge of whom you serve.

Repeat yesterday's meditation on surrender and finish with complete acceptance of yourself as a soul, a child of God. Accept the world as it is with this understanding: 'When I change the world changes … self-transformation brings world transformation.' Your acceptance is the key to knowing God As He Is and For Who He Is, and you become God's helper. Contemplate these thoughts deeply in your three two-minute periods of silence, and hourly throughout the day. They hold the secret to world peace.

51

Knowing myself as All That I Really Am, I see an angel.

Angels are ego-less, true to themselves, and benevolent messengers with no self-interest. They are always depicted as light and reveal the way to God. When we let go of bodily identity and become free of ego and illusion, we know ourselves as All That We Really Are, becoming true to ourselves just like angels.

When you keep a secret, you are hiding the truth from someone. Ego deludes you with falsehood, keeping secret the truth that, really, you are an angel. Ego whispers, 'Know me as I am and I will keep you safe. Holding grievances is my plan for your salvation.' When you recognise God your original, innocent, pure, angelic character begins to emerge and ego dies.

From this day on, see your angelic potential and challenge Maya (ego, illusion). Reveal your spirit to the world and serve humanity with its transparency. Understand that God is changing you, and it is God who is working through your transformation. Continue to surrender today with this awareness, 'Knowing myself as All That I Really Am, I see an angel.' Visualise yourself in a body of light during morning meditation. Imagine yourself healed, revealing love to the world. Fill your body of light with truth, love and wisdom. Imagine you are transparent, revealing these qualities which show the way to God. Repeat this visualisation during your three two-minute periods of silence today and affirm the lesson hourly throughout the day.

52

I serve the world through merciful vision.

$\mathcal{M}$erciful vision is angelic vision. It carries the power of love, understanding and truth. Inner healing is a process of the heart and soul leading us to the truth of All That We Really Are. Through it we gain wisdom, re-emerge our innocence and become love. These three qualities allow us to understand that wrong action is based on wrong understanding, so we cannot judge others. Merciful vision does not challenge wrong action but creates right understanding.

Merciful vision extends the love we receive from God to the world. We become one with God through the sublimation of ego, false truth and wrong identity. Merciful vision on the world is our means of being transparent and allowing God to work through us. What we receive from God we give from God. The giving and receiving are one — nothing separates these. We make the world one with God.

This is complete surrender and the healing of separateness.

⚊ ⚊

In morning meditation today contemplate with detachment on the wrong actions of souls in this world. Forgive them with this thought: 'Knowing not who you are, you know not what you do.' Look at them with clarity, complete understanding and acceptance. Open your heart to these souls so that they may know the truth and the love of God. You will experience yourself becoming an instrument of God because merciful vision draws God's love to the self at the same time as revealing it. Repeat this contemplation in your two-minute periods of silence and affirm the day's lesson hourly.

53

I neither withhold nor direct love.

As we let go of ego and surrender we *become* love. Love is the gift that merciful vision extends to the world. Our angelic nature serves the world by never withholding or directing love. Angels are like 'spiritual roses'. Settled in their own beauty they radiate the colour and fragrance of unconditional love to the world.

A rose is complete in its own beauty and fragrance. It doesn't retreat or withhold its beauty no matter who comes along. Whether others stop to appreciate the rose is their choice. The rose is unconcerned, never giving up its beauty or fragrance. Knowing yourself as All That You Really Are, you become a spiritual rose aware of your own beauty, unconcerned whether anyone notices your qualities and never withholding or directing love. With this degree of self-respect and freedom from fear your love is unconditional and its power reveals truth.

In forty minutes of meditation today visualise yourself as a rose of any colour you choose.

Allow the colour to change during the meditation. Imagine that the colour of the rose represents spirituality and truth and its fragrance is love.

See the colour and fragrance radiating in every direction, touching and changing all who notice it. Imagine others turning into roses of a variety of colours. Together, the world over, you are creating a scene of exquisite beauty and fragrance. Use this imagery in your three periods of silence today and affirm the day's lesson every hour.

54

Love has its own power.

*F*rom the previous lesson we can see that love is quite different from attachment. When we condition love we want it to be reciprocated or to receive some other form of return. We seek to control its direction by determining who is or isn't worthy of love. All this conditioning represents attachment, which comes from fear and ego's desires. We have come to mistrust love, so we condition it and it becomes conditional.

When you let go of fear, attachment and desire you discover that love is an intrinsic quality. You don't have to look for it on the outside, and the less you interfere with it the more powerful it becomes. When you surrender you belong to the source of love and become an instrument of love. Realising that love has its own power you allow it to fill and radiate from you. Love is more real than the world around you and is the quality through which God reveals Himself to others. Unconditional love is a pure state of being, free from attachment, revealing truth.

—◆ ◆—

Repeat yesterday's meditation and exercises with the added dimension of seeing love as an independent energy that reaches everyone in its own way. Affirm to yourself, 'I neither withhold nor direct love. Love has its own power.'

55

Revealing love is my salvation.

*U*nconditional love has one source and one
purpose. It comes from God and reveals God.
To receive it is to be completely healed. Revealing
it is your salvation; your liberation from illusion,
fear and ego. When you reveal the love you receive
from God you become a world server and world
benefactor, and nothing separates you from God.
    When you are offered unconditional love you
adopt it, become it and reveal it simply through
accepting it yourself. Acceptance is the basis of
freedom from ego's dictates and deception. Only
love is real. Accept and reveal love and you will
have salvation.

In your forty minutes of meditation today visualise
God as a point of light radiating love. See this light
reaching you and filling you until nothing separates

you from God's love. Imagine yourself becoming lighter and floating upwards, away from the physical world. Visualise yourself connecting to the light of God, radiating love to the whole world. The world rotates before you and you have a single powerful thought for the healing of all souls. Repeat this imagery in your three periods of silence today and reaffirm hourly: 'I neither withhold nor direct love. Love has its own power. Revealing love is my salvation.'

56

Truth takes me beyond influences.

*T*ruth means knowing ourselves as All That We Are. When we firmly embrace this knowledge we experience self-respect and our mind becomes powerful. We can learn to withdraw from the influence of negativity. We are tolerant, loving, understanding and forgiving, and we accommodate weaknesses. Through truth we have the power to discern, judge and act according to our higher purpose, and our courage and self-confidence allow us to face the world and be transparent.

Be humble and strong. To donate what you have taken from God simply use the power of co-operation. The sense of working with God stops you from being influenced by the weaknesses, attitudes and actions of others. You become a world-server.

In meditation today visualise yourself as powerful, constant and unshakeable. See yourself as beyond the influence of All That Is Not Real and connected to every soul in the world that has ever recognised God. Draw strength and power from this gathering and donate your combined power and strength to the souls of the world who are still blind. Repeat this visualisation in your periods of silence today and affirm hourly, 'Truth takes me beyond influences.'

57

Heaven is coming.

*I*n recognising truth and knowing God's love we look into the mirror of the future where everyone has the divine reflection and colour of God. Heaven awaits its creation. Right now, through our co-operation with the divine, God extends powerful vibrations for world change and transformation.

In meditation today visualise the whole world before you. Go to the trouble spots, the war-torn countries and where natural disasters have occurred. Sense the sorrow of the souls living there and feel that they are calling you. Draw God's presence onto the stage of the world and visualise it as a cocoon of light and safety over the world. Co-operate with this light and imagine that hundreds and thousands are co-operating too, the world over. Create one thought for purity, enlightenment and the end of illusion: 'Heaven is coming. It is our creation.' Repeat this today in your three periods of silence, and hourly throughout the day.

58

It is time to return home.

*R*emembering All That We Are and returning
to innocence is a return to God. It is also our way
home. With God we leave this old world behind
and discover a world of profound peace and blissful
silence. We fill our soul with the power of silence,
and on our way home we transform the world's
sorrow and remove its illusion.

— ◆ —

In meditation today imagine yourself drawn home
to God. Imagine a land of silence and peace in
the heart of God and feel yourself drawn to it.
Let yourself become very tiny until you are an
infinitely small point of light, eternal and simple.
As you are drawn into God, visualise powerful
rays extending back to the world stage, creating
profound peace, and drawing the souls of the
world to you. 'It is time to return home. We are

all going home together.' Repeat this in your three periods of silence, and make it your hourly affirmation throughout the day as a prayer for world peace.

I am as God knows me.

We finish this course as we began — knowing that our true identity is soul. It is the only thing we must remember. Everything else — God, the divine order of the drama, understanding karma, serving humanity and world renewal — follows easily and naturally.

— —

Today remember that you are a very simple point of living energy. Make yourself infinitely small and be drawn home as you were yesterday. This time visualise yourself in front of a tiny bright perfect star, changing your nature to reflect His exactly. Spend your meditation for the day in this way and affirm to yourself, 'To become like You (God) I return Your love. I am as God knows me.' Repeat this in your three periods of silence and hourly throughout the day.

*I now know God as He is and
for who He is.*

All we need to know is that we are souls created
with the purity of God. We fall from innocence
(grace) in the destiny of the drama, separating
ourselves from both our original nature and God's
love. Ultimately we experience ourselves as All
That We Are Not. This contrast allows us to
experience the ultimate joy of rediscovering God
and of recreating ourselves as All That We Are.

❦ ❦

In today's meditation let God fulfil all your relationships. Surrender and let go of everything and
say to God, 'I come to You as my loving Mother.'
Then let God become your archetypal mother,
nurturing your spirit as you merge into the ocean
of love. Then go to God as your father and listen
to His directions. Merge into the ocean of wisdom
and create within yourself a feeling of complete

obedience. Next, go to God as your child. Create within yourself that special love we have for children and give this special love to God. Feel as though you would sacrifice anything for God, just as you would for a child. Create other relationships such as those of friends and companions before finally returning to the lesson of the day. Go to the source of God, the essence from which He radiates. Experience the radiance of all relationships and affirm, 'I now know You as All That You Are and for Who You Are. Thank you, my Lord.' Make this your hourly affirmation and reflect on it in your three periods of silence.

Keep these lessons with you. Repeat them and create the experiences you want. Be simple, be free and enjoy.

Om Shanti

Brahma Kumaris
World Spiritual University

$\mathcal{T}$he Brahma Kumaris World Spiritual University
is an international organisation which teaches
Raja Yoga meditation as a free community service.
It is affiliated with the United Nations as a non-
government organisation with consultative status
in the Economic and Social Council, and has
consultative status in Unicef.

If you want to further develop and practise
the meditation philosophy discussed in this book
you may wish to contact a Raja Yoga centre near
you. The contact numbers of the main centres in
Australia and throughout the world are listed below
for your convenience. As there are over six thousand
centres in the world, the centres listed here can give
you details of other centres that may be close to you.
All teaching is voluntary and most centres run a free
introductory course in meditation. As these contact
details are subject to change, you may prefer to
access the Brahma Kumaris Internet sites at

www.bkwsu.com or www.brahmakumaris.com.au
for a current listing and more information about
the organisation.

Brahma Kumaris main centres

Australia

Australian Capital Territory
Canberra (02) 6260 5525

New South Wales
Ashfield (Sydney) (02) 9716 7066
Leura, Blue Mountains Retreat Centre
    (02) 4784 2500
Newcastle (02) 4942 4060
Wilton Retreat Centre (02) 4630 8124
Wollongong (02) 4227 2241

Queensland
Brisbane (07) 3368 2391
Gold Coast (07) 5530 2690

South Australia
Adelaide (08) 8269 7811

Tasmania
Hobart (03) 6223 5460

Victoria
Baxter (Retreat Centre) (03) 5971 1599
Fitzroy (Melbourne) (03) 9417 4883

Geelong (03) 5243 0530
McKinnon (Melbourne) (03) 9578 9955
North Balwyn (Melbourne) (03) 9857 8871

Western Australia
Perth (08) 9317 4670

Canada
Toronto 1 416 537 3034

China
Hong Kong 852 2806 3008

Fiji
Suva 679 307 799

Ireland
Dublin 353 1 6603 967

Malaysia
Kuala Lumpur 60 3 2282 6396

New Zealand
Auckland 64 9 579 5646
Christchurch 64 3 389 7978
Dunedin 64 3 473 7137
Wellington 64 4 567 0699

Philippines
Manila 63 2 890 7960

Singapore
Singapore 65 467 1742

South Africa
Johannesburg 2711 487 2800

United Kingdom
Cardiff 44 2920 384272
Glasgow 44 141 423 5141
London 44 208 727 3350

United States of America
Atlanta 1 770 939 1480
Boston 1 617 734 1464
Dallas 1 972 478 7089
Los Angeles 1 323 933 2808
Miami 1 305 442 2252
New York 1 516 773 0971
Peace Village Retreat 1 518 589 5000
San Francisco 1 415 563 4459
Washington 1 301 593 4990

Healing Heart and Soul
meditations on compact disk

written by Margaret Pinkerton
set to ambient music and
spoken by Carmen Warrington

*Words don't do justice to the healing you can experience through
each meditation on the CD. These meditations are recommended for
spiritual travellers and for those who are going through trauma or who
have suffered personal loss. When you listen to the CD you embark on
a journey in which you can experience unconditional love and the power
of truth. It can help you heal emotional problems and free your soul.*

Dr Roger Cole, author of *Healing Heart and Soul*

To purchase the CD contact:
Eternity Ink, 1st Floor, 77 Allen Street, Leichhardt NSW 2040
Email: bkmedia@ozemail.com.au
Internet: www.brahmakumaris.com.au

Healing Heart and Soul CDs are $15.00 each plus $5.00 postage and
packing. Send a cheque or postal order for $20.00 to Eternity Ink
to receive your copy of the CD, or complete the credit card
details below and send the signed form to Eternity Ink:

NAME ON CARD _____

Please indicate with a tick:

VISA ☐   BANKCARD ☐   MASTERCARD ☐

CARD NUMBER _____

EXPIRY DATE _____

DEBIT AMOUNT (including postage) $ _____

SIGNATURE _____

TELEPHONE NUMBER _____ (AH)

_____ (BH)

ADDRESS _____

_____

_____